DON'T CHICKEN OUT, EAGLE IN

Soaring Above Fear and Embracing Bold Faith

PELUMI OPEYEMI OYEBOADE

Copyright © 2025 Pelumi Opeyemi Oyeboade
All Rights Reserved

No part of this publication may be reproduced or distributed in any form or by any means without the prior permission of the author and/or publisher.

Kemp House
152 -160 City Road
London, EC1V 2NX
United Kingdom

ISBN: 978-1-917451-89-5
Published by Action Wealth Publishing and Pelumi Oyeboade
Printed in the United Kingdom

Although the author and publisher have made every effort to ensure the accuracy and completeness of information contained in this book, we assume no responsibility for errors, inaccuracies, omissions, or any inconsistency herein. Any slights on people, places, or organisations are unintentional.

The material in this book is provided for educational purposes only. No responsibility for loss occasioned to any person or corporate body acting or refraining to act as a result of reading material in this book can be accepted by the author or publisher.

To my beloved wife, Abiodun Oyeboade. Thank you for believing in the vision long before the first word was penned. Your gentle counsel, contagious optimism, and unfailing love lifted my wings every time fear tried to clip them.

I also dedicate this book to the cherished memory of my parents, Evangelist Joseph Olusegun Oyeboade and Kikelomo Oyedoyin Oyeboade. Your unrelenting prayers, integrity, and example of servant-hearted leadership taught me to stand tall like an eagle and never shrink back. Though you now watch from eternity's vantage, your legacy lives on in every page.

DON'T CHICKEN OUT, EAGLE IN

CONTENTS

ACKNOWLEDGMENTS 1
FOREWORD 3
INTRODUCTION 6
CHAPTER 1: THE CALL TO SOAR: INTRODUCTION TO THE
    "EAGLE IN" MINDSET 11
    Recognizing the Insidious Nature of Fear 12
    The Eagle Versus the Chicken 14
    The Call to Soar: A Moment of Decision 16
    Embracing the Storm as an Ally 17
    The Genesis of Bold Faith 18
    The Importance of Vision 20
    Ordinary Beginnings, Extraordinary Outcomes 21
    The Framework of This Book 22
    Reflection and First Steps 25
    Conclusion: An Invitation to Ascend 26

CHAPTER 2: UNDERSTANDING THE NATURE OF FEAR 29

- The Many Faces of Fear 30
- The Difference Between Healthy Fear and Limiting Fear 33
- Fear Masquerading as Responsibility 34
- Fear's Favorite Playground: Our Thoughts 36
- Practical ways to counter fear-based thoughts: 36
- Why Now? The Timing of Fear 37
- Biblical Perspectives: Fear in Action 38
- Modern Parallels: Everyday People Wrestling with Fear 40
- Fear Is Loud—But Your Calling Is Louder 41
- Practical Tools to Overcome Paralyzing Fear 42
- From Awareness to Action 44
- Bridging to the Next Chapter 45

CHAPTER 3: FACING GIANTS: LESSONS FROM DAVID AND GOLIATH 47

- The Unassuming Shepherd 48
- Identifying Your Goliath 49
- The Power of Preparation in the Pasture 51
- Overcoming Naysayers and Detractors 52
- Faith Over Fear: David's Defining Perspective 54
- A Single Stone: Breaking Down the Battle 55
- Integrating the Interviewee's Story: Defeating Personal Goliaths 56

DON'T CHICKEN OUT, EAGLE IN

The Ripple Effect of a Giant's Defeat 57
Lessons and Takeaways for Facing Your Giants 58
Bridging Faith and Action 60
Reflection: Your Next Battle 61
Transition to the Next Chapter 62
CHAPTER 4: STANDING FIRM IN THE FACE OF ADVERSITY: LESSONS FROM DANIEL 64
Daniel's World: A Culture in Conflict 65
Integrity in Small Things 66
Standing Firm Amid External Pressures 68
The Heart of the Matter: Conviction over Convenience . 70
The Den of Lions: Confronting the Ultimate Threat 71
Practical Wisdom for Today's Lions' Dens 73
Standing Firm in the Interviewee's Journey 74
Personal Reflection: The Cost of Compromise 75
The Fruit of Faithfulness 76
Contemporary Leaders Who Withstood the Lions 76
Practical Steps to Apply Daniel's Lessons 77
Moving Forward: A Life Anchored in Conviction 78
CHAPTER 5: A VOICE OF COURAGE AND ACTION: LESSONS FROM ESTHER 81
Esther's World: A Kingdom Hanging in the Balance 82
The Reality of Risk 83
Transition from Passivity to Purpose 84
Bold Action: Esther's Strategic Banquet 86

Modern Parallels: Voices of Courage 87
Danger and Deliverance: The Outcome 88
Faith in Action: The Interplay Between Fear and Power
.... 89
Practical Lessons from Esther's Boldness 89
Courage Beyond Self-Interest 90
The Power of a Single Voice 91
Esther's Legacy and Ours 92
Reflection and Next Steps 93
Looking Ahead 94
CHAPTER 6: RISING ABOVE CHALLENGES LIKE AN EAGLE 96
The Eagle Mentality 97
Rick Wagoner and GM in 2008: A Corporate Storm 99
Winston Churchill: Rising Above a Nation's Darkest Hour
.... 100
The Biblical Promise: Soaring on Eagles' Wings 102
Using the Storm to Propel You 103
The Risks of Ground-Level Thinking.................................. 104
Storms as Agents of Transformation 105
Applying the Eagle Mentality to Everyday Life 106
Testimonies of Soaring.. 108
Handling the Fear Factor 109
Reflection and Call to Action.. 110
Moving Forward: Embracing the Next Storm 110

DON'T CHICKEN OUT, EAGLE IN

CHAPTER 7: PURPOSE-DRIVEN PERSEVERANCE 113

Defining Purpose-Driven Perseverance 114

Biblical Foundations: Paul's Race of Endurance............ 116

Modern Illustration: Bethany Hamilton 117

The Nigerian Friend: From Heartache to Entrepreneurial Drive... 118

Purpose Beyond Self: Esther and Daniel Revisited 120

Obstacles to Purpose-Driven Perseverance 121

Spiritual Dimensions of Perseverance 122

When Perseverance Seems Impossible: Overcoming "Dark Nights"... 124

The Ripple Effect of Perseverance 125

Practical Examples of Purpose-Driven Perseverance .. 126

Reflection and Next Steps... 127

Conclusion: Embrace the Long Game 129

CHAPTER 8: CULTIVATING RESILIENCE THROUGH COMMUNITY 131

The Myth of the Lone Hero 132

Biblical Example: The Power of Together 133

Why Resilience Needs Community...................................... 134

Our Nigerian Friend's Experience: Community at Work 135

Finding or Building Your Community 136

Nurturing Healthy Community Dynamics........................ 138

Corporate or Professional Communities.......................... 139

The Spiritual Practice of Bearing One Another's Burdens 140
Overcoming Relational Barriers to Community............. 141
Harnessing Technology Wisely 143
The Collective Impact: More Than an Individual Gain . 143
Reflection: Embracing God's Design for Togetherness 145
Closing Thought 146
CHAPTER 9: NAVIGATING TRANSITIONS: LEAPS OF FAITH IN CAREER AND LIFE 147
The Nature of Transition: Risk and Opportunity............ 148
Biblical Foundations: Abraham's Leap into the Unknown 149
Leaps in Career: When to Pivot 150
Life Transitions and Identity Shifts 152
Our Nigerian Friend's Major Leap: Emigrating to the U.S. 153
Strategies for Navigating Transitions with Grace 155
The Emotional Roller Coaster of Transition 156
Modern Parallels and Success Stories 157
Spiritual Anchor: Trust in God's Guidance 159
Overcoming Fear in the "In-Between" 160
Embracing Divine Surprises 161
Conclusion: Step Forward, Rooted in Faith...................... 162

DON'T CHICKEN OUT, EAGLE IN

CHAPTER 10: TAKE THE BULL BY THE HORN: THE POWER OF DECISIVE ACTION 165

Why Action Matters 166

From Intention to Impact: Bridging the Gap 167

The Cost of Inaction 168

Overcoming Barriers to Bold Action 169

Examples from the Modern World 170

Steps to Take the Bull by the Horn 171

Balancing Boldness and Wisdom 172

The Spiritual Fuel for Bold Action 173

Dealing with Critics and Adversity 174

Celebrating Incremental Victories 175

A Word on Endurance 176

Conclusion: Act Now, Rise Higher 177

CHAPTER 11: FAITH IN THE STORM: EMBRACING GOD'S STRENGTH 180

Storms as a Testing Ground for Faith 181

Biblical Threads: Trusting God Amid the Tempest 182

Modern Examples: Faith Under Fire 184

Why Storms Often Deepen Faith 185

Choosing Faith Over Fear 186

Practical Ways to Stand Firm in the Storm 187

Storms and God's Redemptive Power 188

Navigating Long Storms: Patience and Perspective 190

The Role of Prayer and Spiritual Warfare 192

Reflection: Our Nigerian Friend's Take on Faith in the Storm 193
Conclusion: Soaring Above, Not Escaping 193
CHAPTER 12: SOARING FORWARD A BLUEPRINT FOR BOLD LIVING 197
A Recap of the Journey 198
Embracing the "Don't Chicken Out, Eagle In" Mindset. 199
From Knowledge to Practice: Making It Personal 200
Navigating Resistance and Adversity 201
Strengthening Others as You Soar 201
Evaluating and Continuing the Journey 202
Sustaining a Lifestyle of Bold Faith 203
Final Reflections on Our Nigerian Friend's Legacy 203
A Commission to Rise 204
Your Roadmap: Putting It All Together 204
The Continual Call to "Eagle In" 204
Concluding Charge: Rise and Shine 205
Final Benediction 205
AFTERWORD 207
CONCLUSION 208
ABOUT THE AUTHOR 215

DON'T CHICKEN OUT, EAGLE IN

ACKNOWLEDGMENTS

My heartfelt gratitude extends to:

My wonderful siblings, *Olumide Oluwayemi, Tolulope Oluwayemi, Bukunmi Oyeboade,* and *Fiyinfoluwa Oyeboade* whose camaraderie, candid feedback, and humour kept me grounded and inspired.

Rev. Gbenga Kotila, my pastor and mentor, for speaking faith into my life and reminding me that vision without courage is merely day-dreaming.

Deaconess Tola Adeoti and **Brother Kolawole Iyiola** thank you for the countless prayers, late-night calls, and practical support that helped transform ideas into chapters.

The leadership and family of **RCCG Mount Zion Parish, Atlanta, Georgia**—your warmth and consistent encouragement created the safe runway from which this book could take flight.

Centre for Reality International Church, Ibadan, Nigeria, and **Christ Ambassadors Evangelistic Team, Ibadan** your passion for the Gospel and unwavering commitment to raising eagles fuel my own.

To everyone who prayed, proof-read, or simply asked *"How is the book going?"* please know that your kindness is woven into every sentence. May this work inspire you to refuse fear and rise higher.

FOREWORD

Humanity is the fullest expression of God on earth, yet when fear takes root the reality we carry shrinks to almost nothing. *Don't Chicken Out Eagle In* sounds the alarm: the treasures inside you cannot shine while fear shares the same space, and the resources God entrusted to you must never be wasted.

The lives of Esther, Daniel, and David spotlighted in this book prove that ordinary people who partner with courage can shape history. You, too, are an eagle. Eagles are built to rise, not to scratch the ground. Stretch your wings; do the very thing for which you were designed. Wishing to fly achieves little; spreading your wings makes flight inevitable. Refuse to settle for low places. In every generation, sky-conquerors are simply ordinary hearts that refuse ordinary limits. Step out with boldness and turn systems that try to exploit you into platforms you can dominate.

Along your destiny-path no external adversity can stop you; only you can. You cannot "eagle in" until you challenge both yourself and the obstacles before you. Face them squarely what opposes you can become thrust for your ascent. Opposition, correctly interpreted, supplies momentum. Until you take the first decisive step, every promise remains theory. What you refuse to confront you will never conquer, so treat every challenge as raw material for promotion.

Guard the values that will announce you to your generation. Popular opinion is a poor compass. Your friendships are corridors that lead either upward or downward; choose corridors that open toward the light. Walk with the wise, because Proverbs 13:20 warns, "He who walks with the wise becomes wise, but the companion of fools will be destroyed." Your company is quietly sculpting your future.

A dominant theme in these pages is this: never sacrifice the ultimate on the altar of the immediate. Do not let fear shipwreck a destiny that faith and patience were meant to launch. Responding to challenges will birth both courage and wisdom. The greater you is calling answer with choices that build rather than

DON'T CHICKEN OUT, EAGLE IN

choices that break. Courage in action is the bridge between prayer and fulfilment; prayers do not overturn decisions only better decisions do.

May this foreword ignite the confidence to unfold your wings and take the heights reserved for you.

Olugbenga Kotila

INTRODUCTION

Every generation faces its own brand of giant economic uncertainty, cultural pressure, personal loss, the silent ache of "what-if." Yet beneath the headlines and the heartaches, a deeper battle rages: the struggle between the life we were created to live and the life fear tries to confine us to. *Don't Chicken Out Eagle In* is a call to end that stalemate. It is an invitation to trade the ground-level scratchings of caution for the wide-sky confidence of faith.

Why an eagle? Because no other creature illustrates so vividly what happens when adversity and identity collide. While smaller birds scatter at the first rumble of thunder, the eagle rises, turning the storm's fury into an updraft. It climbs higher not in spite of the wind, but because of it. That single image frames every page that follows: storms are not always sent to destroy us; many are meant to carry us to altitudes we could never reach in calm weather.

Across twelve chapters you will journey with biblical trailblazers—David, Daniel, Esther, Jonah, and more—whose stories prove that ordinary people become history shapers when they refuse to bow to fear. You will also meet modern men and women who echo the same theme: Bethany Hamilton, who returned to competitive surfing after losing an arm to a shark; Tim Tebow, who transformed public criticism into fuel for global philanthropy; and a young Nigerian student whose succession of setbacks became a springboard into business, ministry, and cross-cultural influence.

Their settings differ, but their rhythm is the same: recognise fear, confront it with faith-filled action, and watch God transform obstacles into opportunities.

This book is deliberately practical. Each chapter unpacks one facet of courageous living and closes with reflection prompts you can apply immediately whether you are deciding to launch a start-up, mending a fractured relationship, or simply daring to dream again after disappointment. You will learn how to:

- ☐ Identify fear's many disguises (from perfectionism to polite procrastination),
- ☐ Face down "giants" with the same logic David used in the Valley of Elah,
- ☐ Stand firm when cultural currents mock conviction, as Daniel did in Babylon,
- ☐ Convert life's storms into lift, the way eagles and resilient leaders do,
- ☐ Harness community so you suffer *with* companions, never *for* them, and
- ☐ Move from intention to decisive, measurable action because faith that never leaves the planning table is merely wishful thinking.

Along the way you will encounter honest discussions about doubt, burnout, and the "in-between" seasons when clouds linger longer than anticipated. This is not a pep-talk for adrenaline junkies; it is a field guide for ordinary believers who want their Mondays to echo the courage they sing about on Sundays. It holds space for lament as well as victory, for Jonah's detour as well as Esther's bold decree, because authentic faith makes room for both.

DON'T CHICKEN OUT, EAGLE IN

Perhaps you picked up this book because a specific storm is already breaking across your horizon a medical report, a financial free-fall, a relationship on the brink. Or perhaps your life looks stable on the outside, yet you feel a restless tug toward something larger than the routines that currently define you. Whatever your backdrop, the principles ahead converge on one liberating truth: fear only rules the ground you give it. The moment you decide to "eagle in," the balance of power shifts.

Expect to be stretched. Courage rarely feels convenient. But also expect to be surprised by the strength that surfaces when you act in spite of shaking knees; by the allies God positions when you refuse isolation; by the creativity that awakens when comfort zones collapse.

Most of all, expect to rediscover God's unshakable faithfulness. From Genesis to Revelation, and from the slums of Lagos to the boardrooms of London, His signature remains the same: He specialises in lifting ordinary people above circumstances that once seemed immovable.

So, take a breath. Lift your eyes from the ground to the sky. The turbulence you feel may be the very wind designed to carry you.

PELUMI OYEBOADE

As you turn the page, do more than read. *Decide.* Decide that fear will not write your next chapter. Decide to spread the wings God gave you, catch the currents of His promise, and rise. The storm is here. The updraft is waiting.

It is time to soar.

CHAPTER 1

THE CALL TO SOAR

INTRODUCTION TO THE "EAGLE IN" MINDSET

Fear is a silent force. It doesn't announce itself with a roar or a thunderclap but rather with subtle whispers and nudges. It resides inside us, begging for comfort and stability, telling us that risk will only bring us harm.

When faced with an unfamiliar task or an uncertain horizon, fear often suggests the path of least resistance: Stay where you are. This is the "chicken out" mindset, the one that keeps our feet on the ground, refusing to budge from safe territory. But there is a higher perspective, one that sees that the storm looming in the distance can also become the very element that lifts us to new heights. That perspective is the "eagle in" mindset.

This book, *Don't Chicken Out, Eagle In*, explores the transformation from a life bound by fear to one fueled by boldness, resilience, and faith. As we begin this first chapter, we will look at what it means to feel the call to soar and how an "eagle in" mindset distinguishes those who are ready to rise above challenges from those who remain bound by fear. We'll see how men and women throughout history, both in biblical narratives and modern contexts, embodied this mindset and how ordinary individuals can begin to cultivate it in their own lives.

Recognizing the Insidious Nature of Fear

Fear can be cunning. It cloaks itself in logic and caution, suggesting that staying safe is the only rational thing to do. It whispers, "Better not start that business; you might fail," or "Don't speak your mind; you'll only cause conflict."

In moderation, caution can be helpful, and it stops us from diving headlong into genuine peril. But when caution becomes excessive, it mutates into an insidious fear that holds us hostage. Suddenly, the very instincts that were meant to keep us safe end up isolating us from growth.

The call to soar begins with recognizing this distortion. Many people see fear as a permanent blockade, an impassable wall. Yet the biblical stories we will examine throughout this book teach a different perspective: fear can be an indicator that we're on the brink of something transformative. It's often in the presence of fear that our greatest opportunities emerge. David felt fear when facing Goliath; Esther felt fear before approaching the king; Daniel felt fear in a den of lions. All these heroes experienced the shock and tremor of fear. Their triumphs didn't arise from an absence of fear but from a decision to press forward despite it.

In modern contexts, we see athletes, entrepreneurs, or students challenged by that same sense of dread. Consider the struggle of learning advanced mathematics after losing someone who had always been your support system. Fear whispers that the gap is too large, the challenge too immense, so why even try? But that moment of hesitation can be a doorway to a completely new trajectory in life if we are willing to open it.

One of the individuals who shared his story during our research grew up in southwestern Nigeria. His family experienced numerous transitions, including moving from one state to another, losing a parent, and balancing school with entrepreneurial ventures to make ends meet. In the hustle of daily life, he witnessed firsthand how fear could stop someone from stepping up. But he also saw how perseverance bolstered by faith could turn a daunting challenge into an opportunity. Even though he was tempted multiple times to "chicken out," the seeds of an eagle mindset began taking root: If life's storms were inevitable, why not try to ride their wind instead of hiding from the rain?

This perspective shift didn't happen overnight. It came through repeated encounters with his limitations. He struggled with mathematics, especially after losing the parent who'd been tutoring him. He feared failure on exams. He feared disappointing his family. Yet, each hurdle forced him to adapt, to ask for extra tutoring, to get creative with finances by raising poultry or running a small gaming shop. Each time, fear knocked at the door, but he answered not with retreat but with small steps of faith and action.

The Eagle Versus the Chicken

Why use the analogy of an eagle at all? There are many majestic creatures we could explore. Yet the eagle stands out because of one specific characteristic: it uses the very

DON'T CHICKEN OUT, EAGLE IN

force of a storm to rise higher. Instead of fleeing from dark clouds and winds, the eagle sets its wings in a position to catch the updraft. With minimal extra effort, it ascends above the turbulence, gaining a vantage point that no earthbound creature could imagine.

Chicken, on the other hand, are domesticated birds that rarely fly, if ever. They peck at the ground and scurry to the safety of a coop at the first sign of trouble. They are content to remain in familiar territory even if it means they never experience the freedom of the skies. The "chicken out" mindset is precisely the impulse to retreat, avoid risk, and remain confined to what is comfortable.

The "eagle in" mindset asks us to do the opposite. It invites us to see that storms, adversity, and challenges are not punishments but potential catalysts. Challenges become the winds that allow us to soar into previously unreachable altitudes.

This principle is echoed in Scripture, most famously in Isaiah 40:31: "They will soar on wings like eagles; they will run and not grow weary; they will walk and not be faint." It's a promise that supernatural strength and clarity are available for those who choose to rise with faith rather than hide in fear.

The Call to Soar: A Moment of Decision

Every journey toward transformation begins with a call, a pivotal moment that disrupts our status quo. For some, that moment is the loss of a job, the start of a new relationship, a tragedy that shakes our foundations, or even a new opportunity that seems too big and intimidating to handle. Suddenly, we find ourselves standing at a crossroads: we can either opt for safety or venture beyond our comfort zone.

The interviewee from Nigeria mentions that one such "call to soar" hit him during his high school years. His mother had passed away, and with her went the academic support he had so heavily relied on. Suddenly, math, an already challenging subject, became nearly impossible to comprehend. He had every reason to back down, to blame circumstances, or to give up altogether.

Yet, this moment forced him to choose between remaining stuck and letting fear dictate his future or stepping forward, seeking help, trying new approaches, and studying harder than ever. While it might not be as dramatic as facing a literal giant or stepping into a lion's den, the principle is the same. The call often appears as a simple, practical choice, yet it sets the stage for a broader spiritual and emotional journey.

DON'T CHICKEN OUT, EAGLE IN

In the Bible, many heroes encountered their "calls to soar" unexpectedly. David was just sent to deliver food to his brothers when he heard Goliath's taunts. Daniel was living out his faith until a royal decree outlawed prayer to anyone but the king. Esther was fulfilling her royal duties when a genocidal threat forced her to risk her life for her people. In each case, these heroes could have turned away and played it safe. Instead, they recognized the significance of their moment and stepped forward. That choice was the spark of something extraordinary.

Embracing the Storm as an Ally

Fear teaches us that storms are hostile, destructive forces. But the eagle sees the storm differently; it's a highway to the heights. This is counterintuitive for most of us because we're wired to avoid pain and discomfort. Yet, time and again, Scripture and personal experience demonstrate that hardship can be the catalyst for profound growth. Without the storm, the eagle remains at a middling altitude. Without adversity, our spiritual and personal growth often remains shallow.

That's why *Don't Chicken Out, Eagle In* insists on flipping our perspective. Suppose the storm is upon us anyway, whether it's financial strain, academic challenges, or a major life transition. In that case, we can see it as a refining fire rather than an existential threat. The interviewee discovered that every time his family's finances grew tight, a new idea, a new solution, or a new expansion of skills emerged. When the primary breadwinner in the family was gone, it forced him to take on responsibilities that initially seemed terrifying. Yet by acting despite that fear, he discovered capacities for resilience and problem-solving he never knew he possessed.

In the same vein, consider Tim Tebow, who frequently faced skepticism due to his outspoken faith and unconventional playing style. Instead of letting criticism define him, Tebow channeled that pressure into greater determination, launching philanthropic initiatives, focusing on personal discipline, and eventually becoming a role model for many. Did criticism sting him? Certainly, but he pivoted from seeing it as a reason to hide to see it as a catalyst to refine his focus and enlarge his platform.

The Genesis of Bold Faith

At the heart of this "eagle in" mindset is faith. Faith isn't merely the belief that "everything will work out somehow." It is an active trust in a God who is bigger than the storms around us. That trust is often forged in moments when the wind howls fiercest when our strength and intellect reach their limit. It's in those moments that we realize we must rely on a strength beyond ourselves.

For our friend from Nigeria, faith was planted and nurtured from childhood. Attending children's Bible classes, singing in church, and growing up on a campus where his father served as educators exposed him to a strong moral and spiritual environment from an early age. When storms arrived, like losing a parent, struggling academically, and shouldering responsibilities well beyond his years, he drew on this foundation. This doesn't mean he was never afraid or never tempted to give up. It means that during the darkest nights, the seeds of faith gave him just enough hope to try again.

Biblically, David's confidence when he stepped up to Goliath wasn't merely self-assurance that he was a skilled shot with a sling. It was a deep trust that God, who had rescued him from lions and bears in the field, would also rescue him from this new threat. His past experiences of divine aid became the steppingstones to confronting bigger challenges. The same is true for each of us. Rarely do we wake up one day and decide to fight giants if we haven't first faced smaller battles that build our faith.

The Importance of Vision

Another key distinction between the eagle mindset and the chicken mindset is vision. Eagles are renowned for their keen eyesight; they can see with astounding detail from great distances. This clarity is symbolic of the importance of maintaining a forward-looking perspective in life. Those who operate under fear have short sight: they see the immediate dangers and possible pitfalls, and they stop there. Those who embrace an eagle mindset look further; they see the potential outcomes, the reward beyond the risk, and the ways God can move mightily through obedience and courage.

We can take an example from the corporate world. Winston Churchill, though primarily remembered as a political leader, possessed a visionary style that resonates with the eagle's perspective. When Britain stood seemingly alone against a Nazi onslaught, the immediate outlook was devastating.

The simplest decision might have been to negotiate peace and avoid more suffering. But Churchill saw beyond that moment. He envisioned not just the cost of war but also the cost of surrender: the loss of freedom and the darkness that could engulf Europe. His vision beyond the immediate fear galvanized a nation to endure what seemed unendurable. The eagle soared amid bombs and blockades, fueled by a faith in ultimate victory.

When we translate vision to a personal level, it means we're compelled by something bigger than present circumstances. Those challenging nights the young Nigerian man spent studying math or traveling back and forth to manage poultry and gaming businesses were driven by more than just making money. He had a vision of completing his education, becoming self-sufficient, and fulfilling his calling, whatever shape that calling might ultimately take. Without vision, frustration quickly sets in. With vision, you understand that short-term sacrifices pave the way for long-term breakthroughs.

Ordinary Beginnings, Extraordinary Outcomes

A significant thread in this chapter, and indeed, the entire book, is that an eagle mindset doesn't demand extraordinary beginnings. Many of the biblical heroes were ordinary people when we first encountered them: David was a shepherd, Esther an orphan, and Daniel a captive in a foreign land. Their initial circumstances didn't scream "hero," yet we revere them now because they allowed faith to transform them and answered the call to soar.

Likewise, we see this in modern testimonies. Some leaders come from humble beginnings, often marked by financial constraints or limited opportunities. The difference lies in how they respond to fear and adversity. They don't see obstacles as final verdicts but as challenges that call forth new levels of creativity and grit.

We heard echoes of this in the Nigerian interviewee's story. He described how his family members had to juggle teaching jobs, small-scale farming, and entrepreneurial ventures on the side. None of that spelled out a privileged or easy life. Yet it instilled in him a work ethic and resourcefulness that prepared him for even bigger leaps, such as moving to a new country and starting anew.

His story reminds us that you don't need to wait for ideal conditions or a high-level platform to start living with an eagle mindset. You can begin right now with whatever you have, wherever you are. If your current "storm" is related to finances, relationships, or spiritual doubt, you can choose to view it as a training ground.

The Framework of This Book

Don't Chicken Out, Eagle In will delve into various biblical figures, such as David, Daniel, and Esther, as well as modern examples, to show that a life of faith and

DON'T CHICKEN OUT, EAGLE IN

boldness is accessible to anyone. Each chapter focuses on a specific principle or story:

- ☐ The Call to Soar – An introduction to the eagle mindset and a challenge to recognize fear for what it is: an opportunity to elevate.

- ☐ Understanding the Nature of Fear – How fear operates and how we can defy its hold.

- ☐ Facing Giants: Lessons from David – Learning how small faith victories pave the way for giant conquests.

- ☐ Standing Firm: Insights from Daniel – The Necessity of Integrity and Conviction in Hostile Environments.

- ☐ The Power of Bold Action: Esther's Courage – The fusion of planning and fearless determination.

- ☐ Rising Above Challenges Like an Eagle – Embracing the Storm as Our Ally in Achieving Greater Heights.

- ☐ Purpose-Driven Perseverance – Connecting Your Trials to a Broader Sense of Calling.

- ☐ Cultivating Resilience Through Community – Understanding how we need others to sharpen and sustain our "eagle in" mindset.

- ☐ Navigating Transitions: Leaps of Faith in Career and Life – How to handle major life shifts without being crippled by fear.

- ☐ Taking the Bull by the Horn – Why Action Is the Non-Negotiable Ingredient in Overcoming Challenges.

- ☐ Faith in the Storm – Trusting God's Promises and Standing on His Word in Moments of Deepest Uncertainty.

- ☐ Soaring Forward: A Blueprint for Bold Living – A final call to continue practicing the eagle mindset beyond the pages of this book.

By anchoring our exploration in both biblical insights and practical stories, we hope to offer a roadmap that illuminates a path from fearful passivity to confident, purpose-driven living.

We'll weave the story of our Nigerian interviewee throughout the chapters, not as a biography but as a real-time illustration that these principles apply universally. You don't have to be David or Esther to experience a breakthrough. You can be an ordinary person with a spark of faith and an openness to transform adversity into altitude.

DON'T CHICKEN OUT, EAGLE IN

Reflection and First Steps

Before we close this opening chapter, let's pause for a moment of self-reflection. The journey ahead isn't about inflating us with false bravado but about rooting out fear at its core. Ask yourself:

What Are Your Storms?

Is it a financial crisis, a relational struggle, or a personal sense of inadequacy? Please write it down. Confront it directly rather than letting it loom in your subconscious.

Are You Currently in 'Chicken Out' Mode?

If so, there's no shame in admitting it. Acknowledging that you've been reluctant to step forward is the first step to turning that behavior around. Remember, fear is universal, but the response is optional.

Can You Identify a Call to Soar?

Take a look at your current circumstances: Are there opportunities that both scare and intrigue you? A project you've been putting off, a conversation you're avoiding, a dream that won't let you be alone. That may be your invitation to "eagle in."

Who or What Is Your Support System?

Consider family, church community, close friends, or even online mentors you've met. Who can help you stay accountable as you begin to shift your mindset? No eagle flies forever alone; even eagles have mates and nurture their young. Community matters.

With these considerations in mind, you're already taking your first steps toward a bolder life. It starts by observing your fear, naming it, and deciding that it will not have the final say.

Conclusion: An Invitation to Ascend

No one is immune to fear. We might envy the eagles overhead, wishing we, too, could lift off and sail through the sky. However, the truth is that the mindset that allows us to soar isn't limited to those with special genetics or privileged circumstances.

It belongs to anyone willing to look at a storm and see more than darkness. It belongs to anyone who, like David, believes that past victories with lions and bears point to a future victory over giants. It belongs to anyone who, like Esther, understands that they are alive "for such a time as this." It belongs to ordinary individuals, like our Nigerian friends, who recognize that the demands of daily life can be a step toward deeper faith

DON'T CHICKEN OUT, EAGLE IN

and resilience if approached with openness and determination.

In the chapters to come, we will delve deeper into the specifics, from understanding the intricacies of fear to learning how to activate faith in the face of adversity. We'll see how our vantage point determines whether the storm crushes us or elevates us. We'll walk through pages of Scripture and pages of living testimonies, showing that *Don't Chicken Out, Eagle In* is a life-altering call to boldness.

If you're reading these words and feeling a stir within you, take heart. That very feeling might be your call to soar. Fear wants to keep you grounded; faith and courage want to lift you. The invitation stands: Do you want to scurry to the coop with the chickens or risk the winds with the eagles? The choice is yours. And if you choose to spread your wings, remember that storms aren't the end of your journey. They might be your runway to greater heights.

So, welcome to the beginning. Let this be the moment you decide fear will no longer be your master. Let this be the chapter in your life where you discover that you, too, can learn to fly above the storm. It won't be without difficulty, and it won't be without moments when you feel the force of the wind pushing against you. But as you hold steady, guided by faith and powered by resilience, you'll find yourself soaring beyond what you once believed possible.

The sky is waiting. Let's ascend.

CHAPTER 2

UNDERSTANDING THE NATURE OF FEAR

Fear. It is one of the most universal human experiences. It whispers, it shouts, it lurks in the back of our minds, and at times, it demands to be the loudest voice in the room. Whether you are standing on the cusp of a new relationship, considering a career shift, facing a difficult exam, or waiting in a waiting room anticipating medical results, fear often shows up unannounced and unwelcome.

In our quest to adopt an "eagle in" mindset, we must confront this intangible force and determine what it is, how it operates, and how we can prevent it from hindering our potential.

Previously, we introduced the idea that storms and the fears they trigger can help us ascend if approached with the right perspective. But before we learn to harness storms, we must first dissect the nature of fear itself. What is fear at its core? Why does it appear at the most pivotal moments? And how can we discern between caution that protects us and paralyzing fear that stifles our growth?

This chapter delves deeply into the anatomy of fear. We will examine the difference between healthy fear, which signals legitimate danger, and limiting fear, which often masquerades as "common sense" or "responsibility" but keeps us from walking through the doors of opportunity. We will also explore how biblical heroes and everyday individuals, such as our Nigerian friend, who is trying to balance family obligations and academic challenges, navigate these distinctions. By the end of this chapter, you should have a clearer picture of how fear operates in your own life and be better equipped to stand firm when its haunting whispers threaten to hold you back.

The Many Faces of Fear

Fear wears many masks. Sometimes, it appears as dread, an ominous feeling that something terrible is about to happen. Sometimes, it disguises itself as overthinking, caution, or "realism." Fear can also cloak itself in the human tendency to procrastinate, telling us we are too busy or ill-prepared to move forward just yet.

Doubt

Doubt often begins with a "What ifs?" *What if I fail? What if this decision backfires? What if I'm not good enough, strong enough, or talented enough?* Although it can appear in fleeting moments, doubt can harden into a persistent sense of unworthiness or uncertainty. The biblical character Moses wrestled with this when God asked him to confront Pharaoh. He asked, in essence, "Who am I to do this?" That "who am I?" is the language of doubt, a direct spawn of fear that tries to keep us inert.

Insecurity

Insecurity lies at the intersection of self-worth and capability. It whispers that your accomplishments are mere accidents or that your best will never measure up. It uses comparisons. Look *at how easily they do it; you could never match that.* In biblical narratives, people like Gideon battled insecurity, often referring to themselves as the least in their families or tribes. Modern contexts are rife with comparisons, especially in the digital age of social media. Each scrolling feed can stoke that gnawing question: *Why am I not more like them?*

Indecision

One of fear's most subtle manifestations is indecision. Instead of shouting, "Stop!" it teases us with endless "Maybe…" scenarios: *Maybe I should wait. Maybe the market isn't ready. Maybe next year will be better.* Paralysis by analysis is the result of extended stasis in the face of possible choices. Often, it's fear of the unknown disguised as "research" or "prudence."

Perfectionism

Perfectionism is another face of fear less obvious than panic but just as inhibiting. When we cannot bear the thought of less-than-ideal results, we often avoid starting altogether. Fear of making mistakes or looking foolish can undermine our ability to progress. We get stuck in endless cycles of preparation, never actually launching our vision, product, or dream.

Each of these variations of fear shares a common root: an inner alarm that says, "You can't handle the consequences." The message is that stepping forward will cost more than you can afford, and you should prioritize your protection at all costs even if it means missing out on something incredible.

DON'T CHICKEN OUT, EAGLE IN

The Difference Between Healthy Fear and Limiting Fear

It's essential to recognize that fear isn't always negative. We have a God-given survival instinct that keeps us from walking into oncoming traffic or sticking our hands in a fire. This *healthy fear* is tied to legitimate danger and prompts a constructive response to protect ourselves and others. If a lion is prowling outside, locking your door and staying inside is common sense, not cowardice.

However, *limiting fear* is the kind that appears to be cautious on the surface, but it confines us to a self-made prison. It amplifies risks, undervalues our capabilities, and overlooks the fact that God can work powerfully through our weaknesses. This fear doesn't just protect us from real danger; it also keeps us from blessings. It's the voice saying, *'Don't speak up; no one wants to hear your ideas,'* or *'You're too old for a new career.' Just accept where you are.*

Healthy Fear (Caution):

- Signals actual danger or threat.
- Motivates us to take protective measures that preserve life and well-being.

- Encourages prudent actions, such as wearing a seatbelt, locking doors at night, or avoiding toxic relationships.

- Typically temporary, dissipating when the threat is resolved.

Limiting Fear (Paralyzing or Overblown):

- Exaggerates possible threats, spinning narratives of worst-case scenarios.

- Prefers indefinite avoidance over constructive engagement.

- Framed as caution or "wisdom," but it works to keep us stuck.

- Does not dissipate easily because it's not purely logical; it's fueled by insecurity and doubt.

Fear Masquerading as Responsibility

One of the most devastating disguises of limiting fear is the veil of "responsibility." Sometimes, especially for those in leadership or breadwinning roles, the fear of failing to meet the expectations of a spouse, children, congregation, or business can be rationalized as simply *being responsible*. To an extent, being responsible is noble. The question is: responsible to what? When genuine responsibility slides into risk aversion, the result is often crippling indecision or stagnation.

Take the example of the Nigerian interviewee who lost his mother in high school and suddenly bore greater responsibility for his siblings. He could have told himself, 'I need to play it safe; I can't afford to mess up because others rely on me.' That mindset could have led him to drop out of his advanced math coursework or avoid entrepreneurial ventures altogether. Instead, he chose to interpret responsibility as *finding a way to move forward and provide solutions.* That shift turned fear into fuel, an energy source that drove him to juggle school, poultry farming, and eventually a small gaming business to finance his education. He still felt fear about failing, but he didn't let fear override genuine responsibilities, such as ensuring the family's financial stability.

Biblically, consider Nehemiah, who felt compelled to rebuild the wall of Jerusalem. He had every reason to fear personal harm or King Artaxerxes' disapproval. But he recognized that responsibility can be a call to courageous action, not to cower.

If Nehemiah had allowed fear to masquerade as responsible caution *I don't want to lose my position in the king's court; the Jewish people might resent my interference anyway* the walls may never have been rebuilt. Instead, he pressed through fear, took a bold stand, and changed history.

Fear's Favorite Playground: Our Thoughts

Fear is a mind game. The apostle Paul captures this dynamic in 2 Corinthians 10:5, where he exhorts believers to "take captive every thought." Thoughts are the primary battlefield where fear wages its war, planting seeds of negativity and letting them grow if unchecked.

A vivid illustration might be you're on the verge of relocating to a new city. Fear might whisper, 'Moving is expensive. ' *You'll be lonely. You'll fail to secure a decent job.* With repetition, these concerns no longer feel like fleeting questions but realities. The mind begins to accept them as truth, influencing our decisions and paralyzing our willingness to take a leap.

Practical ways to counter fear-based thoughts:

Name the Fear: Saying aloud, "I'm afraid that I won't find a job," helps dissipate the fog. Naming something concretely transforms it from an amorphous dread into an issue you can address.

DON'T CHICKEN OUT, EAGLE IN

Challenge the Fear: Ask yourself, *Is this fear realistic? Is it guaranteed?* Often, the worst scenario is far from guaranteed.

Seek Evidence: If possible, gather the information that counters fear. For instance, research the job market in your new city. Talk with locals or potential employers. Fear hates verified information. It thrives on speculation.

Pray and Reflect: The spiritual discipline of bringing fears before God, journaling them, and seeking divine perspective can clarify which fears are legitimate warnings and which are limiting illusions.

Why Now? The Timing of Fear

Fear has a knack for showing up precisely when opportunities knock. Promotions, relationships, new business ventures, or relocations often trigger fresh waves of anxiety. Why? Because change is inherently uncertain. The larger the potential reward, the more substantial the risk.

This phenomenon appears in Scripture repeatedly. When the Israelites stood at the brink of the Promised Land, ten of the twelve scouts returned with fearful reports of giants. They acknowledged the land's abundance but fixated on the dangers, turning the entire nation back toward the wilderness. The timing of that fear was no coincidence. It surfaced at the threshold of a breakthrough. The same pattern continues today in big and small ways.

Big Decision Fear: This often manifests at life's major crossroads, such as new jobs, engagements, or relocations.

Incremental Progress Fear: Even smaller, day-to-day decisions can spark fear, such as launching a small website, volunteering at church, or starting a side hustle. The moment we try to move beyond comfort, fear tries to reel us back.

Recognizing the timing of fear can be empowering. Once you learn that fear tends to intensify when you stand at the edge of growth, you stop being surprised by it. You can even reinterpret it as a clue you're on the right track if fear is rising; maybe it's because you're crossing into territory that genuinely matters.

Biblical Perspectives: Fear in Action

A. Adam and Eve

The Garden of Eden provides the first biblical snapshot of fear. After they ate from the forbidden tree, Adam and Eve hid. Fear gave birth to shame, or perhaps shame gave birth to fear; either way, they ran from God.

DON'T CHICKEN OUT, EAGLE IN

Human history's earliest depiction of sin underscores how fear drives separation, secrecy, and evasion. Their fear was tied to the possibility of divine judgment. Instead of openly confessing, they allowed fear to dictate the narrative, which led to blame-shifting and a relational rupture.

B. Elijah

Elijah is a fascinating study of the timing of fear. After one of the most spectacular miracles in Scripture calls down fire on Mount Carmel, he receives word that Jezebel wants to kill him. Exhausted and drained, fear overtakes him, and he flees into the wilderness, convinced that he is alone and that all is lost. A mighty prophet, who had just earlier witnessed God's power manifest in flames, succumbs to despair. This story shows that even strong leaders can crumble under the right conditions of stress and fatigue. God's response, significantly, is not condemnation but restoration; providing Elijah with food, rest, and a fresh encounter with God's presence.

C. Peter

Peter's moment of fear is famously captured when he attempts to walk on water. Initially, his eyes are on Jesus, and he steps onto the waves in faith. But fear creeps in as he notices the wind and waves, and he begins to sink. Jesus asks, "Why did you doubt?" highlighting how quickly fear can replace faith when circumstances look threatening.

In each of these biblical vignettes, fear leads to hiding, exhaustion, or sinking. However, the presence of fear wasn't the final word. God consistently offers a way through or a re-centering of focus.

Modern Parallels: Everyday People Wrestling with Fear

In addition to biblical examples, modern stories also reveal the enduring pattern of fear. Our Nigerian friend, who found himself juggling multiple family and academic responsibilities after losing his mother, confronted many forms of fear. One particularly vivid scenario involved math class. Already challenging for him, mathematics became doubly daunting without his mother's support. Fear whispered, 'What if I fail?' *I don't have anyone to guide me now.*

For a period, he battled indecision about whether to continue advanced math courses or switch to something simpler. But ultimately, he recognized that the real danger was not academic failure; it was the limiting belief that he could not adapt or excel. He sought extra tutoring, took advantage of after-school sessions, and persevered. Over time, what started as crippling fear turned into a motivating factor. The result? He eventually passed his exams, even if it required multiple attempts.

In a Western context, we observe similar patterns among entrepreneurs who hesitate to launch a startup due to fear of financial ruin and among working professionals who refuse to change jobs for fear of leaving the familiar behind. Fear rarely looks the same twice, but its fingerprint is clear: it halts us at the doorway of possibility.

Fear Is Loud—But Your Calling Is Louder

If there is a single truth to remember as you encounter the many forms of fear, it is this: fear may be loud, but your calling can be louder. When you allow the passion and vision God has placed in your heart to speak as forcefully as fear does, you begin to recalibrate your internal volume dials.

Consider Esther. Presented with a life-and-death choice to speak up for her people, fear surely roared in her mind: *You could die! It's not your business to meddle in politics. You're only queen by circumstance.* But who *knows but that you have come to your royal position for such a time as this?* Spoke louder, compelling her to move forward.

In your own life, ask:

- ☐ What is God calling you toward?
- ☐ Is it a business idea, a ministry role, a career shift, or a leap of faith in relationships?
- ☐ What are the loudest "What if?" statements in your head?

Write them down. Now, for each "What if?" consider a faith-filled rebuttal: *What if God makes a way? What if this is an open door for a deeper purpose?*

Are you hiding behind the guise of responsibility or pragmatism?

Sometimes, your future success depends on taking a risk for short-term comfort in exchange for a long-term destiny.

Practical Tools to Overcome Paralyzing Fear

Identify and Name It

Half the battle is recognizing when fear is the root cause of indecision or avoidance. Please give it a name, such as fear of failure, fear of rejection, fear of financial ruin, or fear of disappointing others, and record it. There is power in calling fear out from the shadows.

Interrogate the Fear

Ask, *"What is the absolute worst that could happen if I try?"* Often, even the "worst case" is something we can recover from. Then, ask, *"What is the best that could happen if I move forward?"* This perspective helps place risk and reward on the same scale.

Seek Mentorship and Counsel

God often uses community to fortify us. Seek out people who've traversed similar paths. Our Nigerian friend found mentors who tutored him in mathematics and guided him through the complexities of running small businesses. Whether in academia, ministry, or entrepreneurship, you may find guidance that clarifies risks and opportunities, thereby lessening the grip of fear.

Small Steps, Big Faith

Overcoming fear doesn't always mean taking a giant leap. Often, it's a series of small, deliberate actions that gradually build momentum. If you feel called to start a business but fear the financial risk, consider taking small steps: develop a business plan, conduct market research, or test the idea on a limited scale. Each micro-action can weaken fear's hold.

Spiritual Practices

Prayer, worship, and meditation on Scripture are powerful for recalibrating your perspective. Passages like Psalm 27:1 ("The Lord is my light and my salvation whom shall I fear?") or Psalm 56:3 ("When I am afraid, I put my trust in you") remind us that fear does not get the final say when our trust is in God.

Embrace Accountability

Confide in someone about the steps you plan to take. Knowing that a friend or mentor is expecting updates can motivate you to move past paralyzing thoughts. The early disciples often went out in pairs there is strength and encouragement in mutual accountability.

From Awareness to Action

As you conclude this chapter, you might feel a new awareness of fear's many disguises. Perhaps you recognize it now in your second-guessing before a big meeting or in your reluctance to call a friend with whom you've had a falling out. Maybe you see it in the excessive way you plan every minute detail of a situation to avoid any uncertainty. Awareness is the first step, but awareness alone is insufficient to break fear's hold. You must move toward action.

Why do you take action? Because fear is allergic to forward movement. Once you commit to a course of action, however small, fear's momentum begins to wane. It might still be present, but it no longer governs your every step. Recall that Peter, even though he began to sink, took those first steps on water. Despite his misstep, he experienced a miracle most of us only dream of, and he grew in faith and understanding. Had he never stepped out of the boat, he wouldn't have learned the difference between focusing on the storm and focusing on Jesus.

Bridging to the Next Chapter

In the next section of this journey, we will look at how *facing giants* like David did with Goliath further illustrates the power of confronting the "impossible." David's story shows us that the size of the enemy is no match for the size of our faith.

Yet before we reach that peak moment of victory, Chapter 2 asks us to do something foundational: unmask fear. Know it. Understand it. Recognize it as a force that can be turned either into a cautionary alert (healthy fear) or a self-sabotaging blockade (limiting fear).

PELUMI OYEBOADE

Our interviewee from Nigeria eventually moved beyond fear's grasp in many areas, shifting to new academic pursuits, starting side businesses, and continuing his faith journey. This progression didn't happen because fear evaporated. It happened because, through awareness and action, he refused to let fear be the defining voice in his story.

Remember: Fear is loud, but your calling is louder. If you let it, the voice of purpose and destiny will outshout the "what ifs" and the "not enoughs." Instead of letting fear stamp your life with timidity, let the knowledge of its nature empower you. Once you see fear for what it is, you can navigate it more confidently and respond with faith and determination.

CHAPTER 3

FACING GIANTS:

LESSONS FROM DAVID AND GOLIATH

Storms are not the only challenge we face in life. Sometimes, the obstacle before us seems less like shifting winds and more like a towering giant blocking our path and mocking our potential. It could be a seemingly unbreakable habit, an intimidating boss, a financial crisis, a major health issue, or anything that looms so large it makes us feel small. The story of David and Goliath famously shows us that what appears invincible to human eyes may be vulnerable when confronted by faith and boldness.

In the previous chapters, we explored the "call to soar" (the eagle mindset) and the subtle nature of fear.

We identified how fear can masquerade as practicality or caution, paralyzing our dreams and aspirations.

Now, in Chapter 3, we delve into one of the most iconic biblical accounts of facing fear head-on: David's confrontation with Goliath. More than a children's Sunday School story, this encounter offers universal lessons about faith, small victories, and the power of a heart that trusts God. We will also examine modern parallels, from high-profile figures like Tim Tebow and Cristiano Ronaldo to everyday experiences, such as our Nigerian friend juggling personal tragedy and academic hurdles, all of which show that true courage doesn't stem from perfect conditions but from a willingness to meet giants in the valley.

The Unassuming Shepherd

David was never supposed to be the one on the battlefield. When the prophet Samuel came to anoint a new king from among Jesse's sons, David, the youngest child, was overlooked, tending sheep in the fields. Even when Israel's army faced the Philistines, David was sent mainly to deliver food to his older brothers and gather news. He wasn't the soldier in shining armor; he was, by all outward appearances, "just a shepherd boy." Yet God saw something else: a heart that trusted Him above all.

DON'T CHICKEN OUT, EAGLE IN

In many ways, this resonates with stories of people who grew up in humble circumstances yet found themselves confronting formidable challenges. Recall the interviewee from Nigeria, who had no illusions of grandeur: he was trying to help his family get by. Like David, who honed his skills protecting sheep from predators, our friend developed resilience by handling smaller challenges, helping with chores, managing the family's poultry, and grappling with tough math courses. These incremental "victories" prepared him for bigger battles later, just as David's encounters with lions and bears paved the way for taking on Goliath.

Key Insight: God often grows our capacity through ordinary tasks in unremarkable places. By tending sheep diligently, David learned bravery and trust in God. By juggling chores and entrepreneurial activities, our interviewee developed an entrepreneurial spirit and discipline. Neither situation appeared grand on the surface, but both were forging the character needed for future giants.

Identifying Your Goliath

The biblical account takes a dramatic turn when Goliath, a Philistine champion nearly ten feet tall, steps onto the battlefield. For forty days, he taunted Israel's armies, challenging anyone to a one-on-one fight. The entire army of Israel, including King Saul, cowered in fear. Goliath's size, weaponry, and relentless mockery created a climate of fear and intimidation.

Modern "Goliaths" can feel just as oppressive. Perhaps it's a crippling student loan debt, a deep-seated fear of public speaking, or a toxic work environment that no one seems willing to address. Like Goliath, these giants can show up day after day, reminding us of our perceived inadequacies. They seem impossible to defeat, so we avoid confrontation and hope the problem will resolve itself on its own.

However, the truth is that ignoring a giant does nothing to diminish its stature. If anything, it grows bolder. The first step to defeating a giant is to name it, acknowledging that it looms large and that its intimidation is real.

When Tim Tebow stepped onto the football field, critics questioned everything from his throwing mechanics to his public expressions of faith. That criticism was his Goliath: an obstacle designed to make him second-guess his identity and abilities. He addressed it not by running from scrutiny but by continuing to speak openly about his beliefs and striving to perfect his craft.

DON'T CHICKEN OUT, EAGLE IN

Reflect: Can you identify a persistent challenge that currently dominates your life? It may be internal, such as insecurity or procrastination, or external, like a failing business or unresolved family conflict. Whatever it is, identify it clearly and acknowledge its power. Only then can you begin to strategize its downfall.

The Power of Preparation in the Pasture

When David volunteered to fight Goliath, Saul initially rejected him. How could a boy with no battlefield experience take on a giant warrior? David's confidence, however, didn't stem from naive optimism; it was grounded in the *small victories* he had already won. He told Saul about his past battles with lions and bears while tending his father's flock. No one saw these private triumphs, but they built David's faith and skill.

We often underestimate the power of past "small wins." Each time you solve a challenging problem, take a leap of faith, or navigate a family crisis successfully, you accumulate testimonies of resilience. When our Nigerian friend managed the family's poultry business, balancing finances and day-to-day operations, he had no idea he was training for more complex responsibilities in adulthood. Similarly, if you've handled minor conflicts at work or persevered in finishing small projects, you're developing mental and spiritual muscle for bigger challenges.

Practical Point:

Keep a Victory Log: Journaling ways you've seen God show up in past challenges can serve as a personal "slingshot." When giants come, you can pull from that reservoir of confidence.

Use Your Unique Skills: David used a sling and stones, unconventional weapons by the standards of the day. Don't force yourself into someone else's armor (like Saul's heavy gear). Utilize your unique strengths, whether it's a distinctive speaking style, innovative technology, or an unconventional approach to problem-solving.

Overcoming Naysayers and Detractors

As soon as David voiced his willingness to fight, he encountered a chorus of doubt. His brothers mocked him, insinuating he was seeking attention. King Saul, after initially objecting, tried to fit David into his armor. This phenomenon is all too common. The moment you decide to confront a significant figure in your life, you may encounter pushback from family, friends, or authority figures. They might say, "You're in over your head," or "That's not how we do things here."

DON'T CHICKEN OUT, EAGLE IN

It's reminiscent of Cristiano Ronaldo's early career struggles. Coming from the relatively small island of Madeira, he faced skepticism regarding his ability to adapt to top-tier football in Lisbon and later in Manchester. Critics questioned his flamboyant style and worried he wouldn't "fit" into more traditional teams. Like David, Ronaldo stuck to what made him effective: hard work, innovation, and an unorthodox approach, and ultimately overcame the naysayers.

To adopt an eagle mindset in the face of giant obstacles, you'll likely need to tune out voices that sow doubt. This doesn't mean ignoring wise counsel. It means discerning the difference between helpful advice and fear-based criticism. David accepted King Saul's blessing but not his armor. He recognized that if he fought the Philistine using somebody else's methods, he would lose.

Action Step: Take a moment to consider who in your life acts as a "naysayer" or "detractor." Could they be well-intentioned but misguided, or are they genuinely undermining your confidence? Sometimes, you can address the root of their concern; other times, you have to proceed, trusting God to validate your calling.

Faith Over Fear: David's Defining Perspective

David's most radical asset was his perspective. He didn't size up Goliath against himself; he sized up Goliath against *God*. To David, Goliath was merely a mortal who dared to mock the living God. That perspective shift transforms challenges. Instead of thinking, *I must have enough strength,* you think, *God is strong enough, and He's with me.*

This is where the true essence of biblical faith emerges. It isn't reckless or baseless confidence. It is rooted in the character of God, who has proven faithful time and again. If you've experienced God's help in smaller issues, you develop an expectation that He can handle bigger ones. Many people flounder because they focus on their limitations. David reminds us to focus on God's limitless power instead.

Modern Parallel: In a world that often scoffs at open displays of faith, Tim Tebow's unwavering stance exemplifies a David-like perspective. When criticized, he frequently points to a higher purpose, framing athletic success as secondary to living out his faith. Many question whether referencing God so openly is wise or relevant, but, like David, Tebow doesn't waver. His confidence isn't in personal prowess alone; it's anchored in a belief that God is involved in every facet of life, including sports.

Reflection: Where do you fix your gaze when confronted by something intimidating on your track record or on the truth that God stands bigger than any giant?

A Single Stone: Breaking Down the Battle

The moment arrives: David rushes toward Goliath with a sling and five smooth stones. He only needs one. That lone stone, guided by David's faith and skill, strikes Goliath on the forehead, toppling the giant. It's over in an instant. While the lead-up is fraught with tension, the actual battle ends quickly once David takes decisive action.

This decisive moment underscores a critical principle: action, fueled by faith, can overcome a seemingly insurmountable obstacle more quickly than we imagine. Often, what prolongs the fight is our hesitation or refusal to confront the giant. Once we commit and trust, the giant's downfall can be abrupt.

Small Tools, Big Impact: David's sling was a simple shepherd's tool. Yet, in the hands of someone practiced and faithful, it became mightier than a sword or spear. In everyday life, your "single stone" might be a well-researched pitch, a bold conversation with a mentor, or a single phone call that changes your trajectory.

Momentum Favors the Bold: After David's victory, the Israelite army found its courage and routed the Philistines. Courage can be contagious. Sometimes, all it takes is one action to spark a chain reaction in your environment.

Integrating the Interviewee's Story: Defeating Personal Goliaths

Let's return to our Nigerian friend's journey and examine how these principles were applied in a real-life context. His "Goliaths" weren't literal warriors but daunting life circumstances:

Financial Strain: Following the loss of his mother, the family's financial responsibilities increased dramatically. Fear suggested it was impossible to keep up with educational costs. Yet he took bold steps in learning small-scale poultry farming, running a mini gaming shop, and odd job. Each effort felt like a "stone in the sling," perhaps small, individually, but collectively powerful.

Academic Challenges (Math Struggles): Many people avoid tough subjects due to fear of failure. He initially wavered but then chose to step up to extra tutoring sessions, retake crucial exams, and persist until he passed. He faced ridicule from people saying, "Maybe you're just not cut out for this." But like David, he trusted that his past small victories, such as passing other subjects and growing in problem-solving, indicated he had more capacity than he realized.

Cultural Transition: Later, he faced a giant in the form of relocating to the United States. Fear insisted that the move was too risky: a new culture, a different academic system, and potential job insecurity. But believing that God could guide him, he approached the opportunity with the same determined faith. Although it required navigating complex paperwork and unfamiliar social norms, he pressed on.

In each case, the key was not sophistication but a willingness to confront the challenge head-on with the resources at hand. He continued to demonstrate that small, faith-infused steps can topple giants over time.

The Ripple Effect of a Giant's Defeat

When David slew Goliath, he didn't merely secure his victory. He liberated an entire nation from intimidation. The Israelites, emboldened by David's success, charged forward to win the battle against the Philistines. Similarly, overcoming a significant challenge in your life often extends beyond personal gain. It inspires those around you.

Consider Tim Tebow's philanthropic efforts: the same boldness that led him to stand firm in public also propelled him to establish charitable foundations and speak hope into challenging situations. Ronaldo's relentless pursuit of excellence hasn't just earned him awards; it has influenced aspiring athletes worldwide to push beyond limitations. Your victory over a health crisis, a financial meltdown, or a toxic work situation can inspire hope in friends, coworkers, or family members who witness you navigating adversity with grace.

Question: Whom might your victory set free? Sometimes, the giant stands in your way not just to block you but to discourage everyone observing you. Your stepping forward can unleash courage in others who are silently fighting similar battles.

Lessons and Takeaways for Facing Your Giants

Acknowledge the Giant

Like the Israelite army, you may have spent days, months, or years ignoring a glaring issue. Break that cycle by calling the giant out *of financial debt, toxic relationships, crippling anxiety, crippling self-doubt, etc.*

DON'T CHICKEN OUT, EAGLE IN

Review Past Victories

Remember the "lions and bears' you've already conquered, whether that's overcoming a childhood hardship, completing a challenging project, or bouncing back from a setback. These smaller victories fortify your faith.

Fight with Your Strengths

Don't assume you have to become a carbon copy of someone else to win. David tried on Saul's armor and found it unworkable. Identify the gifts and tools that have proven effective in your life.

Expect Naysayers

Not everyone will believe in your calling or your approach. Be prepared. Discern whether their advice is wise counsel or fear in disguise.

Lean on God's Power, Not Your Own

Shifting the focus from *I must be strong* to *God is strong in me* changes how you approach any obstacle. That posture opens the door for miracles, both large and small.

Act Decisively

Delayed action often magnifies the giant's psychological hold. Once you have clarity, don't procrastinate. Move with the swiftness of David running to the battle line.

Remember the Aftermath

When giants fall, entire communities can be liberated. Your courage can become a catalyst for others to find their strength and step into their battles with renewed hope.

Bridging Faith and Action

Faith without works, as the apostle James says, is dead. David's faith was visible not just in his words, *"Who is this uncircumcised Philistine...?"* but in his actions: stepping onto the battlefield with a sling in hand. If you sense God urging you to start a new venture, speak up for someone who's voiceless, or apply for a role that feels beyond your qualifications, do more than pray about it. Prayer is vital, but it should propel you toward action, not replace it.

Take Ronaldo's trajectory once more. Physical talent alone didn't shape him into a global phenomenon. He trained relentlessly, adopting strict diet and fitness regimens that some doubted he could maintain. That discipline is reminiscent of David's spiritual discipline, practicing the sling until it became second nature. The unstoppable partnership of discipline plus divine favor is a hallmark of giant slayers, whether in sports, academia, business, or spiritual life.

Reflection: Your Next Battle

Before we move on to the next chapter, pause and reflect:

☐ Identify One Giant You're Facing Right Now

It might be a major project at work, a relational crisis, or an addiction you've tried to break. Please write it down.

☐ Recall Your Lions and Bears

List at least three personal victories, no matter how small, that demonstrate times you pushed through adversity. Connect the dots: those experiences built resilience that can help you now.

☐ Assess Your Sling and Stones

What tools or resources are already in your hands? Consider your natural talents, acquired skills, networks, or supportive relationships. These might be more potent than you realize.

☐ Plan a Decisive First Step

Don't get bogged down in hypotheticals. Identify one concrete action to take within the next week, such as sending an email, requesting a meeting, initiating a conversation, or investigating a resource.

☐ Pray Boldly

Bring your fear and plans before God, asking for courage and clarity. Allow spiritual conviction to fuel your resolve. Remember: David's confidence was anchored in the truth that the battle belongs to the Lord.

Transition to the Next Chapter

In this chapter, we've watched David rise above the crowd's timidity to confront a giant that paralyzed an entire nation. We've also seen how everyday individuals, from Nigerian students to modern athletes, channel a similar spirit to face their personal Goliaths. The essence of the eagle mindset shines through again: adversity, when met with faith, can propel us higher than we ever dreamed possible.

Next, we'll explore another biblical hero who stood firm under pressure, Daniel. While David's story shows us how to step onto the battlefield and strike down giants, Daniel's story highlights unwavering integrity in the face of cultural and political adversity. Sometimes, our greatest challenge isn't a single giant but an environment that slowly demands we compromise our values. Whether you're confronting a lion in a den or a giant in a valley, the principle remains: those who trust in God and act courageously find that obstacles turn into catalysts for growth.

Let this be a reminder: the giant that looms so large right now can fall faster than you imagine once you decide to face it. The real giant killer is faith in a God who transcends our perceived limits.

As you close the pages of this chapter, may you carry a renewed sense of confidence: you were never meant to cower under the shadow of Goliath. With God's guidance and your active participation, even the mightiest giants must bow. The same David, who stood as a shepherd boy on a battlefield, later became a king, an outcome that only God could have foreseen. Perhaps, as you face your giant, you, too, stand on the threshold of a destiny far grander than you dare to believe.

Go forth boldly. Let your sling and stone be guided by the unwavering conviction that no challenge, no giant, is bigger than the One who empowers you. Your "Goliath moment" might be the turning point that reveals the warrior and the future leader within you.

CHAPTER 4

STANDING FIRM IN THE FACE OF ADVERSITY:

LESSONS FROM DANIEL

When adversity strikes, our immediate instincts can vary from fight to flight. But there is another, subtler response that often defines who we become: standing firm. This isn't the bluster of aggression or the paralysis of fear; rather, it's the calm, rooted conviction that certain values and beliefs are worth protecting at any cost—even in the face of overwhelming pressure. The biblical story of Daniel offers us a masterclass in standing firm under intense scrutiny, political machinations, and the threat of dire consequences.

DON'T CHICKEN OUT, EAGLE IN

Now we dig into what it takes to remain steadfast, especially when the pressure to compromise is immense. Daniel's story is not just a historical footnote about a faithful Israelite in a foreign empire; it's a vivid example of how integrity, discipline, and divine trust converge to overcome intimidation. As always, we will weave in modern parallels from high-profile figures in sports or entertainment to the everyday adversities that our Nigerian friend encountered. Through these stories, we see how standing firm can transform adversity into a proving ground for faith, character, and leadership.

Daniel's World: A Culture in Conflict

When Jerusalem fell to Babylon, Daniel then a young man was taken into captivity. Torn from his homeland, he found himself thrust into the opulent, foreign world of King Nebuchadnezzar's court. The Babylonian empire was a place of competing gods, lavish feasts, and strict hierarchies. Daniel, renamed Belteshazzar by the royal officials, was enrolled in an elite program to train in the literature, language, and customs of the empire.

Right away, we see that Daniel's faith and cultural identity are at risk. The Babylonians weren't just content to conquer Jerusalem physically; they wanted to reshape the minds and loyalties of the best and brightest Jewish captives. Yet Daniel and his friends (Hananiah, Mishael, and Azariah) had been raised to worship the God of Israel a belief system diametrically opposed to the polytheistic, idol-worshipping traditions of Babylon.

Key Tension: Would Daniel compromise his convictions to fit into Babylonian society, or would he remain true to God's commands at the risk of losing status, comfort, or even his life?

This tension resonates with our modern experiences. While many of us don't live in literal exile, we inhabit professional or social environments that sometimes run contrary to the values we hold dear. For example, we may work in companies that prioritize profit above all else, pressuring employees to skirt ethical lines. Or we may be part of social circles that mock religious devotion or moral boundaries, making us feel like aliens in our own city.

In such climates, the call to stand firm is both daunting and essential. Daniel's journey reveals how to navigate cultural conflict without losing oneself.

Integrity in Small Things

One of Daniel's first recorded tests involves food. Assigned a daily portion from the king's table which likely included foods forbidden by Jewish law Daniel

DON'T CHICKEN OUT, EAGLE IN

requested a diet of vegetables and water. This might seem minor compared to facing lions or interpreting dreams, but it encapsulates a big principle: integrity in small things paves the way for faithfulness in greater trials.

Why Food? Food was part of Babylon's assimilation strategy. Eating from the king's table was a symbolic acceptance of Babylon's gods and culture. Daniel knew that giving in here even if it seemed harmless could erode the foundation of his identity.

Risk and Resourcefulness: Daniel didn't rebel loudly or cause a scene. He respectfully proposed a ten-day trial for him and his friends. When their health flourished, they gained the goodwill of their superiors and proved that devotion to God could coexist with serving in a pagan court.

This principle comes to life in contemporary settings. Many of our moral and spiritual compromises aren't about grand gestures but about small, everyday decisions: fudging numbers in a financial report, telling a "white lie" to appease someone, or joining in gossip about a colleague.

Our Nigerian friend found this out when he started multiple small businesses (such as a poultry farm and gaming shop) to finance his education. Surrounded by peers who sometimes cut corners whether illegally selling products or evading taxes he had to decide whether short-term gains were worth long-term corruption of character. Like Daniel, he chose integrity, even if it meant slower progress.

Takeaway: Standing firm is often cultivated in the small, overlooked choices. If we can be faithful in lesser matters, we strengthen our capacity to face down larger tests of faith and principle.

Standing Firm Amid External Pressures

As Daniel rose through the ranks of Babylon's advisors, he inevitably attracted both favor and jealousy. In Daniel 6, he finds himself under King Darius, facing a political scheme designed to trap him. The officials who envied Daniel's competence and integrity convinced the king to issue a decree that no one could pray to any god or man except the king for thirty days. The penalty for disobedience? The lion's den.

This is where the story becomes especially dramatic. Daniel faced a binary choice: stop praying to his God or risk a gruesome death. He chose the latter, continuing his practice of praying three times a day, in plain sight, with windows open toward Jerusalem. For Daniel, ceasing to pray or hiding his faith was not an option. He was respectful of authority, but not at the expense of his ultimate loyalty to God.

Modern Parallels

Workplace Policies: In some corporate cultures, discussing faith or personal beliefs is frowned upon, leading to subtle or overt pressures to "tone it down" or hide convictions. Standing firm doesn't require defiance for defiance's sake, but it may mean politely declining to engage in activities that violate personal integrity.

Public Figures: Celebrities and athletes who openly share their faith often face backlash. Yet many stand firm, using their platforms to speak about values that matter to them. Like Daniel, they risk social "lions" being canceled, mocked, or losing endorsements because they believe in a higher calling.

Think About: What form do your "lions" take? Are they societal norms that pressure you to conform? Are they industry standards that clash with your morals? Recognizing these modern lions is the first step in preparing to face them.

The Heart of the Matter: Conviction over Convenience

Daniel's unwavering stance wasn't born of stubbornness; it sprang from deep conviction. He understood that his true identity and allegiance lay with God, not Babylon. This concept of *conviction over convenience* is vital in any context.

Conviction: A firmly held belief that shapes actions regardless of outcome. For Daniel, it was a devotion to God's laws. For others, it might be a commitment to honesty, compassion, or social justice.

Convenience: Actions dictated by immediate comfort, ease, or appeasement of authority or culture. This is where short-term pragmatism can derail long-term integrity.

Our Nigerian friend encountered a conviction-versus-convenience dilemma when he had to weigh short-term survival like quickly making more money against moral boundaries. Watching peers engage in dubious practices to get "quick cash," he realized that sacrificing his principles for immediate benefit would be short-sighted. Instead, he chose a slower but more sustainable path, trusting God's provision. Much like Daniel, he found that consistent integrity eventually earned him trust and respect, opening doors he never anticipated.

Practical Tip: Regularly evaluate your decisions by asking, "Am I acting out of conviction, or is this merely convenient in the moment?" This simple question can illuminate whether fear or faith drives you.

The Den of Lions: Confronting the Ultimate Threat

Despite Daniel's faithfulness, the consequences were severe. He was thrown into the lion's den a literal death sentence. From a human standpoint, no outcome other than death was likely. But Daniel's God, the same God he prayed today in and day out, intervened by sending an angel to shut the lions' mouths.

This astonishing deliverance is a reminder that standing firm does not guarantee an easy path, but it does open the door to divine intervention. Sometimes, we're saved from the lions in dramatic fashion; other times, God's intervention comes in quieter forms, like giving us strength to endure or granting us favor with unexpected allies. Regardless, Daniel's miracle underscores that the final word belongs to God, not our adversaries or circumstances.

PELUMI OYEBOADE

Contemporary Echoes

Jim Caviezel: An actor who faced significant industry pushback for openly sharing his Christian faith and starring in religious films. In interviews, he recounted health scares (including being struck by lightning during filming) and professional risks. While not literally thrown into a den of lions, he experienced a cultural "den" where standing firm carried consequences.

Christiano Ronaldo: Though not typically cited for faith-based conflicts, he has faced intense media scrutiny, personal hardships, and pressure to conform to the spotlight's expectations. In certain moments like championing charitable causes or speaking openly about personal values he risked alienating fans or sponsors. But by holding to his personal convictions (commitment to family, discipline, philanthropic efforts), he modeled a stance of integrity under intense public pressure.

In each case, as with Daniel, the refusal to compromise eventually yields a deeper sense of credibility and respect. Even King Darius ended up praising Daniel's God once he witnessed Daniel's miraculous survival an ironic twist that highlights how a single person's stand can shift the atmosphere in unexpected ways.

DON'T CHICKEN OUT, EAGLE IN

Practical Wisdom for Today's Lions' Dens

Daniel's experience, though set in ancient Babylon, presents timeless strategies for those navigating hostile or morally ambiguous environments:

Cultivate Daily Disciplines Daniel's habit of praying three times a day kept him aligned with God, rather than with the shifting whims of Babylonian society. Whether it's morning devotions, journaling, or mindful silence, consistent spiritual (or moral) practices anchor us when adversity hits.

Be Excellent in Your Work Daniel stood out for his exceptional skill, intellect, and integrity. This combination earned him favor from successive kings. If you perform with excellence, not only do you glorify God, but you also disarm critics who might otherwise attack your faith or convictions.

Form Strategic Alliances Daniel did not stand alone; he had friends like Shadrach, Meshach, and Abednego who shared his faith. Community support is critical. Seek out people at work, church, or in your neighborhood who understand your values and can encourage you.

Maintain Respect Even in Dissent Daniel disagreed with certain edicts, but he was never disrespectful toward authorities. Polite, firm dissent often resonates more powerfully than aggression. It can catch adversaries off guard and cultivate favor in unexpected places.

Trust God's Sovereignty Ultimately, Daniel's hope wasn't in his own cleverness but in God's supremacy. Whether we talk about corporate layoffs or personal betrayals, we might not fully control outcomes, but we can maintain a posture that trusts in divine guidance and care.

Standing Firm in the Interviewee's Journey

Our Nigerian friend had his own version of a "lion's den" when he moved to the United States. Facing culture shock, high expectations, and potential discrimination, he had to decide whether to alter his identity his faith, his accent, his background to fit in. For instance, some suggested he downplay his strong Christian beliefs so as not to alienate potential employers or neighbors. Yet he chose to remain transparent about his convictions.

In one instance, he had a job opportunity that clashed with his desire to be actively involved in a church community. The job demanded near-constant availability, including weekends. It was tempting he needed the income. But he felt strongly about setting aside time for worship and fellowship, so he respectfully declined. Initially, this seemed like a lost opportunity, but within weeks, another door opened: a position that allowed more flexibility and ended up being a better fit for his skills. His story illustrates that, like Daniel, standing firm may incur an immediate cost but often leads to unexpected provision.

Personal Reflection: The Cost of Compromise

While standing firm can inspire others and lead to miraculous turnarounds, compromise is often the path of least resistance and the one we choose more frequently than we'd care to admit. Consider how easily we tell small lies to avoid conflict or keep silent when witnessing injustice. Each compromise chips away at our core, making it easier to compromise again next time.

Journaling Prompt: Write about a time you compromised on something you believed in. How did you feel afterwards? Did it resolve the situation, or did it create a lingering sense of regret or misalignment within you?

Sometimes, it's these small "misalignments" that accumulate into a life we barely recognize a life where we feel we're going through the motions, lacking passion or purpose. Daniel's model challenges us to do the opposite: to keep the small daily commitments that maintain our alignment with who we are called to be.

The Fruit of Faithfulness

By the end of Daniel's story in the lion's den, he emerges unscathed. Astonished, King Darius issues a decree that Daniel's God should be revered throughout the kingdom. This outcome is as shocking as it is instructive. When we stand firm, we not only secure our own integrity; we also become catalysts for change in our environment.

Visibility of Faith: Daniel's faith wasn't hidden. It was public enough that others knew exactly how to target him. Yet that same visibility became a testimony of divine power.

Transformation of Culture: Darius's decree hints at how one act of courage can ripple outward, influencing policies, hearts, and minds.

Elevation and Endurance: After this ordeal, Daniel continued to prosper under Darius and later under King Cyrus. Faithfulness can lead to long-lasting influence.

Contemporary Leaders Who Withstood the Lions

Let's briefly spotlight a couple of modern examples that echo Daniel's resilience:

DON'T CHICKEN OUT, EAGLE IN

Patricia Heaton: Known for her roles in "Everybody Loves Raymond" and "The Middle," Heaton has publicly shared her Christian faith and pro-life stance in an industry often critical of such views. While she's faced online hostility and professional risks, she continues to speak openly, refusing to compromise her convictions for broader acceptance.

Chad Veach: Pastor of Zoe Church in Los Angeles, Veach stands firm in biblical teachings even in a city that can be cynical about organized religion. He's maintained a consistent message that merges cultural relevance with scriptural authenticity, navigating both fans and critics in a manner reminiscent of Daniel's respectful steadfastness.

Their stories, like Daniel's, reveal that adversity be it in entertainment or ministry does not automatically mandate compromise. Instead, adversity can highlight the authenticity of our faith and the depth of our moral resolve.

Practical Steps to Apply Daniel's Lessons

Identify Your Core Non-Negotiables Make a list of values or convictions you refuse to sacrifice integrity, faith, family commitments, etc. Having these explicitly stated helps when you face "gray area" decisions.

Establish Daily Devotional Habits Whether it's prayer, meditation, reading Scripture, or quiet reflection, consistency nurtures an internal compass that stands firm when chaos roars.

Communicate Boundaries Upfront If you sense that a job or relationship might eventually test your boundaries, clarify your position early. This fosters respect and reduces surprises later.

Seek a Trusted Community Daniel had friends who shared his beliefs. Find like-minded individuals or mentors who can support and pray for you when pressure mounts.

Prepare for Consequences Standing firm may come at a cost. Mentally accept that relationships might shift, or opportunities might close. However, trust that God can open better doors aligned with your calling.

Stay Humble and Respectful Standing firm doesn't mean arrogance. Daniel's humility and tact played a role in his survival. Even when we firmly disagree with a system or person, we can do so graciously.

Moving Forward: A Life Anchored in Conviction

Standing firm in the face of adversity is neither glamorous nor easy. It often unfolds in private battles of conscience and in public moments of trial. Yet the reward is profound: a life that remains true to its God-given purpose, unshaken by cultural currents or intimidating circumstances. Daniel's story teaches us that adversity can become a crucible for deeper trust in God refining who we are and how we lead.

What's striking about Daniel is not just one isolated act of faith (praying despite a decree) but a lifestyle of unwavering commitment. Each chapter of his life from the early dietary test to the lion's den demonstrates a consistent posture of fidelity. This consistency is what sets apart truly resilient individuals. They aren't heroic for a moment; they carry steadfastness across seasons, forging a reputation for reliability, honesty, and grace.

As you wrap up this chapter, consider your own lions be they cultural pressures, toxic workplace policies, or personal temptations. Reflect on Daniel's example:

- He never let the environment dictate his identity.
- He recognized small compromises lead to bigger ones.
- He trusted God's power more than any threat wielded by earthly kings.

That same trust can guide you through challenges large and small. You might not be thrown into a den of actual lions, but you may face equally daunting tests of loyalty and courage. When you stand firm rooted in faith, guided by integrity you not only honor God but also become a beacon of hope for those who witness your journey.

In the next chapter, we'll shift our focus to Esther a figure who took bold action in a moment of national crisis. Where Daniel exemplifies steadfastness in the midst of systemic pressure, Esther teaches us how to raise our voices and take decisive steps when it truly matters.

Both stories illustrate that the "Don't Chicken Out, Eagle In" mandate isn't confined to a single method. Whether through patient endurance or bold initiative, faith can triumph over fear if we're willing to stand our ground and do what's right.

You have a purpose. You have convictions worth defending. And like Daniel, you have access to a divine strength that surpasses every earthly threat. Let Daniel's witness encourage you: if you remain faithful in the small things and unyielding before the lions, you may find that adversity becomes the very stage upon which your faith and God's glory shines brightest.

CHAPTER 5

A VOICE OF COURAGE AND ACTION:

LESSONS FROM ESTHER

For those who feel uncertain, overlooked, or caught in impossible circumstances, Esther's story offers a powerful reminder: sometimes, *you* are the answer you've been waiting for. Where Daniel demonstrates steadfast faith under systemic oppression, Esther's narrative highlights bold intervention in a life-or-death crisis. She did not merely stand firm she *stepped forward* and used her position to protect an entire nation. In doing so, she exemplifies the principle that faith, courage, and humility can merge into decisive action capable of altering the course of history.

In this chapter, we shift our focus from surviving adversity to *actively confronting* it. If the previous chapters taught us to face giants (David) and stand firm (Daniel), Esther pushes us one step further: to take audacious action when the time is right.

We will see how Esther's willingness to risk her position, her comfort, and even her life resonates with the challenges we face today whether it's a single parent advocating for their child, a community leader confronting social injustice, or an entrepreneur launching a risky but meaningful venture. Along the way, modern testimonies and reflections from our Nigerian friend's journey will underscore that courage isn't limited to ancient monarchies. It's an ever-present invitation to move from hesitance into boldness.

Esther's World: A Kingdom Hanging in the Balance

The Book of Esther paints a vivid backdrop of royal intrigue in the Persian Empire under King Xerxes (also known as Ahasuerus). The king, easily swayed by advisers and prone to lavish displays of wealth and power, deposed his first queen, Vashti, for refusing his command. Into this volatile court steps Esther: a young Jewish woman raised by her cousin Mordecai.

DON'T CHICKEN OUT, EAGLE IN

Initially, Esther ascends to the throne by winning a beauty contest seemingly a passive, external process over which she has no real power. Yet as the story progresses, we see a remarkable transformation. She goes from a timid young woman hiding her Jewish identity to an advocate willing to expose herself to tremendous risk for her people.

Key Challenge: When Haman, a high-ranking official, orchestrates a plot to annihilate the Jews, Esther faces a decision: remain silent and safe, or leverage her influence with the king to stop the genocide. The problem? Approaching the king without being summoned can be punishable by death. Nevertheless, Mordecai poses the chillingly relevant question: "Who knows whether you have come to the kingdom for such a time as this?" (Esther 4:14). In other words, *Esther, maybe you're exactly where you are so you can act.*

The Reality of Risk

Esther's dilemma is not just an ancient drama. It mirrors the modern tension we face when confronted by a crisis that demands action. She lived in a society where even a queen could be executed for offending royal protocol. For many of us, the stakes differ but the fear is similar. We worry that speaking up might cost us friendships, opportunities, or employment. We doubt if we have enough credibility, resources, or courage to tackle our "Haman" head-on.

In the corporate world, a mid-level manager might discover unethical practices within their organization. Reporting these issues could jeopardize their job or career trajectory. Yet, as Mordecai's words echo: *Could it be that this person is exactly where they are for such a moment?* If they remain silent, countless employees or consumers might be harmed. If they speak out, they risk retribution.

Esther shows us that courage isn't about being fearless; it's about acting despite fear. She famously requests that the Jewish community fast and pray with her for three days before she enters the king's presence. This spiritual preparation reminds us that true bravery draws from a source deeper than mere adrenaline an alignment with divine purpose, a collective sense of mission, and the unwavering belief that doing right is worth the cost.

Transition from Passivity to Purpose

Before Esther's defining moment, Scripture doesn't record any heroic acts on her part. She's obedient to Mordecai's instructions to conceal her Jewish identity

DON'T CHICKEN OUT, EAGLE IN

and cooperates with the royal procedures. But the crisis thrusts her into a moral and spiritual crossroads. Mordecai's pointed question "If you remain silent at this time, relief and deliverance will arise for the Jews from another place... And who knows whether you have not attained royalty for such a time as this?" forces Esther to confront the reality that passivity is itself a decision.

Lessons:

Position Is Not Accidental. Whether you're a student, a stay-at-home parent, a CEO, or a volunteer, the sphere you occupy might be your mission field.

Past Silence Doesn't Preclude Future Boldness. Even if you've kept your head down until now, you can still rise to the occasion when needed.

Divine Timing. Esther arrived in the palace "coincidentally" after Vashti's deposition. But there are no true coincidences when it comes to God's purposes.

Mordecai's words are a clarion call that resonates with the "Don't Chicken Out, Eagle In" ethos. When a pivotal moment arrives, you may be exactly where you need to be even if that place seems unlikely or uncomfortable.

Bold Action: Esther's Strategic Banquet

Esther's approach to King Xerxes is a blueprint for courage fused with wisdom. She doesn't barge in accusing him or Haman of wrongdoing. Instead, she invites the king and Haman to a banquet twice. This patient, strategic approach does several things:

It Demonstrates Respect. Despite having every reason to be outraged, Esther maintains a posture of respect and humility.

It Builds Anticipation. By holding *two* banquets, she creates curiosity in the king's mind, ensuring she has his full attention.

It Minimizes Hostility. Confronting Haman publicly or rashly might have provoked immediate retaliation. Instead, Esther masterfully unveils the plot at the right moment, with the king prepared to hear her.

For us, "taking the bull by the horns" doesn't always mean an all-out confrontation. Sometimes, it involves strategic conversations, thoughtful planning, or building alliances before exposing wrongdoing. Consider a whistleblower who gathers evidence carefully before going public, or an activist who engages in dialogue with community leaders prior to staging a protest.

DON'T CHICKEN OUT, EAGLE IN

Esther's example teaches that boldness and patience are not mutually exclusive; they can operate hand in hand to achieve impactful results.

Modern Parallels: Voices of Courage

Bethany Hamilton: The professional surfer who lost her arm in a shark attack exemplifies action despite fear. While her story isn't about dismantling a genocide plot, her return to competitive surfing became a "voice of courage" for those wrestling with trauma and disability. She used her platform to inspire thousands, paralleling Esther's use of her queenly platform to save her people.

Tim Tebow: Facing criticism and mockery for his open expressions of faith, Tebow consistently takes action launching philanthropic projects, speaking at youth events, and using his public image to bring awareness to causes like adoption and human trafficking. Instead of merely complaining about adversity, he acts, much like Esther, to leverage his influence for a higher cause.

Our Nigerian Friend: Though not a queen in a palace, he confronted moments where his leadership and convictions made a difference such as leading a campus fellowship or working with local communities. Once, he helped mediate a conflict between two student groups that threatened campus harmony. Despite fears of backlash, he organized meetings, listened to grievances, and brought them together for dialogue. It resembled Esther's strategic banquets: action taken at the right time, with a spirit of unity, ultimately defusing a volatile situation.

Danger and Deliverance: The Outcome

Esther's moment arrives at the second banquet: she reveals her Jewish identity and Haman's plot to the king. Xerxes, appalled at this betrayal against his queen and her people, orders Haman's execution. Further steps are taken to empower the Jews to defend themselves, averting the planned genocide. Ultimately, an entire people group is saved because one woman chose to risk her life for a greater good.

A critical note: Esther's victory isn't a passive "miracle" dropped from heaven. It's a divine orchestration *through* human courage and planning. Yes, God is sovereign. But Esther had to speak. Mordecai had to challenge her. The Jewish community had to fast and pray. The synergy between divine favor and human responsibility is at the heart of many breakthroughs even now.

DON'T CHICKEN OUT, EAGLE IN

Reflection: Is there a crisis in your environment personal or communal that requires a bold voice? What would happen if you dared to speak up, even if the cost feels high?

Faith in Action: The Interplay Between Fear and Power

Esther undoubtedly felt fear; her first response to Mordecai's plea was essentially, *Don't you know I could die if I go unsummoned before the king?* Yet she acted anyway, bolstered by prayer and communal support. This story solidifies the principle: *fear does not disqualify you from being used by God.* Indeed, moments of fear can be the very crucible in which courage is forged.

Many of us want to eliminate fear before taking action. We wait for perfect conditions or absolute certainty. But Esther's approach demonstrates that bravery is choosing to move forward when the reasons to stay silent are most compelling.

Practical Lessons from Esther's Boldness

Build Alliances Esther relied on Mordecai's wisdom and the collective prayer of the Jewish community. Who in your life can pray, strategize, or support you as you step out of your comfort zone?

Prepare Spiritually Fasting and prayer were crucial to Esther's plan. Whether you're facing a board presentation, a legal battle, or a difficult family meeting, don't neglect spiritual preparation asking God for discernment, favor, and protection.

Leverage Influence Wisely Your platform might be social media, a local community board, or your position at work. Like Esther, consider how you can use this influence strategically for good rather than purely for personal gain.

Know the Right Time Esther waited until the second banquet to reveal her request. Patience can enhance the impact of courage. Rushing prematurely might sabotage the cause; waiting too long may forfeit the moment.

Accept Potential Loss Courage often comes at a cost. Esther had to settle the possibility that she might perish. Likewise, you may lose certain comforts, relationships, or opportunities by acting on your convictions. Yet the potential outcome saving lives or affecting true change often justifies the risk.

Courage Beyond Self-Interest

One of the most striking elements of Esther's story is her willingness to put her own life on the line for others. Her situation as queen might have afforded her personal safety, at least temporarily. But she recognized that her calling transcended self-preservation.

Application: In a world often consumed by individual ambition, Esther's selfless courage invites us to consider how our actions might benefit those beyond our immediate circle. Could it be an advocacy for marginalized people in your city, or offering mentorship to youth who lack role models? When we activate Esther-like courage, we step into a divine narrative that extends our influence to help the vulnerable and powerless.

The Power of a Single Voice

Esther's voice changed the fate of a nation. This underscores a recurring theme in "Don't Chicken Out, Eagle In": *one individual's boldness can ripple across entire communities.*

Cultural Shifts: Often begin with a single voice challenging the norm. Think of Martin Luther King Jr., Nelson Mandela, or Malala Yousafzai each championed causes with personal risk, echoing Esther's willingness to speak despite danger.

Organizational Change: A single whistleblower can revolutionize a company's ethics. A single teacher can transform a school's culture by standing against bullying.

Family Breakthroughs: In many families, one person's decision to end a cycle of abuse or addiction can liberate future generations. That choice demands the same kind of courage Esther showed in the Persian court.

If you ever catch yourself thinking, "I'm just one person; my voice won't matter," remember Esther. Her example defies that notion, reminding us that God often uses a solitary voice to ignite widespread transformation.

Esther's Legacy and Ours

After the Jews triumphed over Haman's evil edict, they established the festival of Purim, commemorating their deliverance. To this day, Purim is celebrated within the Jewish community as a reminder of God's faithfulness and Esther's courageous role. Her legacy is thus woven into the cultural and religious fabric of an entire people.

What about our legacy? Few of us will alter the course of nations in a single stroke, but our actions still leave echoes. Maybe your bold stand at a local school board meeting ensures safer policies for children. Perhaps your willingness to speak out about discrimination in the workplace paves the way for equal treatment of future employees. Or your advocacy for mental health resources in your church might break the silence and stigma for countless individuals.

Esther's story beckons us to ask: *What legacy of courage and compassion are you building?* It doesn't require a royal crown to make a lasting impact—just a heart responsive to the needs around you and a willingness to risk personal comfort.

Reflection and Next Steps

Identify a Cause or Crisis Ask yourself: Is there a looming issue personal, communal, or global that burdens your heart? Like Esther, maybe you've been positioned to respond.

Discern Timing Before rushing in, pray or reflect: *Is this the moment? How do I prepare?* Seek wise counsel, gather information, and consider strategic steps that reduce unnecessary resistance.

Embrace Fear as a Catalyst If you feel afraid, that may be confirmation that the matter is significant. Engage friends or mentors who can support you through fasting, prayer, or simple moral backing.

Speak with Clarity and Respect When you voice concerns whether to a boss, a public official, or family members model Esther's respectful approach. Emotional rants rarely yield fruitful outcomes. A measured, thoughtful proposal often carries more weight.

Trust in Divine Intervention Esther didn't see the end from the beginning. She didn't have a signed guarantee that Xerxes would spare her. Yet she trusted God enough to move forward. Let that faith be an anchor—knowing that even if the outcome doesn't match your initial hopes, stepping out in obedience can yield unforeseen blessings.

Looking Ahead

Having explored Esther's model of courageous action, we're reminded that transformation often hinges on a single decision to remain silent or to speak, to stay hidden or to step out. Faithfulness in adversity, as we saw with Daniel, lays the groundwork for bold actions like Esther's. Together, these stories reiterate the book's core message: Fear is not the victor unless we yield to it. We can indeed "soar" above our challenges if we embrace faith and purpose.

As we continue our journey through *Don't Chicken Out, Eagle In*, the next chapters will delve deeper into how adversity, when met with an eagle mindset, can actually *lift* us, just as storms lift the eagle to higher altitudes.

DON'T CHICKEN OUT, EAGLE IN

We'll also discuss practical strategies for "taking the bull by the horns" the active pursuit of growth, excellence, and resilience that characterizes lives of significance. Esther's bold pivot reminds us that waiting for perfect conditions can be an excuse, and sometimes the only thing standing between us and destiny is the willingness to say, "If I perish, I perish, but I must act."

Be encouraged: The time for silence is over if you see injustice, neglect, or the need for reform in your circles. You might be the voice that saves a family, a business, or an entire community from devastation. And as Esther shows, you don't need extraordinary pedigree or background only a heart attentive to God's call and a willingness to risk for the greater good. Your courageous action could be the pivot point for a story of deliverance, redemption, or revival.

In the final analysis, Esther's story isn't merely about one woman's bravery; it's about how an entire nation was rescued because that woman refused to stay silent. May her example embolden you to take that step you've been hesitating about knowing that you, too, might have come to your position *for such a time as this.*

CHAPTER 6

RISING ABOVE CHALLENGES LIKE AN EAGLE

Eagles are unique among birds for their instinctive response to storms: rather than fleeing from them, they use the turbulent winds to ascend higher than ever before. Where smaller birds scurry for cover, the eagle spreads its wings, catching the updraft that thunderstorms create, and soars above the clouds. This chapter focuses on how we, too, can "rise above" life's storms. Rather than succumbing to adversity, we can leverage challenges to gain new perspective, resilience, and a deeper reliance on God.

Having explored how David confronted a giant, how Daniel stood firm in the lion's den, and how Esther took bold, strategic action to save her people, we now turn to another biblical metaphor: the eagle a symbol of strength, clarity of vision, and the capacity to capitalize on adversity.

And just as we have seen modern parallels in sports figures, entrepreneurs, and ordinary people, we will highlight contemporary examples like Winston Churchill in World War II, GM's Rick Wagoner during the 2008 financial crisis, and our Nigerian friend's personal transitions to show that you, too, can take flight on stormy winds instead of remaining trapped below them.

The Eagle Mentality

The eagle's approach to a storm is often cited as a powerful illustration for faith, courage, and resilience. While other birds (and many of us) see a storm and feel dread, the eagle sees an opportunity to ride an updraft to higher altitudes.

It's an almost perfect picture of Isaiah 40:31: "But those who wait on the Lord shall renew their strength; they shall mount up with wings like eagles..."

Key Insight: The *eagle mentality* looks at adversity not as a final threat but as a potential ally for growth. This is not naïve positivity; it's an active decision to confront difficulty with faith and vision, expecting God to use storms for elevation.

A Two-Fold Mindset

Embrace the Wind: The eagle doesn't create the storm, but it uses what's already there. Similarly, we rarely get to choose our storms financial crises, sudden job losses, health challenges but we can decide how we respond.

Aim for a Higher Altitude: The eagle gains a perspective above the clouds. From that vantage, obstacles below seem smaller. In our challenges, "rising above" allows us to see solutions and insights that aren't visible at ground level.

Our Nigerian friend mentioned that each family crisis like losing his mother or relocating to a new state forced him to rely on God more deeply and develop skills (business management, academic perseverance) that later proved invaluable. Though these storms felt terrifying, they lifted him to a place of greater maturity, resourcefulness, and spiritual depth.

DON'T CHICKEN OUT, EAGLE IN

Rick Wagoner and GM in 2008: A Corporate Storm

In 2008, the global financial crisis hit the automotive industry especially hard. General Motors (GM), one of America's iconic companies, stood at the brink of bankruptcy. Its CEO at the time, Rick Wagoner, faced an unprecedented storm: plummeting sales, a rapidly changing consumer environment, and a global recession. Many predicted GM's complete collapse.

How Did Wagoner Rise Above?

Facing Reality: He didn't deny the severity of the crisis. Instead, he acknowledged the scale of GM's debt, inefficiencies, and the urgent need to restructure.

Seeking Support: Realizing the company needed both public and private assistance, Wagoner worked with government leaders to secure a bailout controversial at the time but ultimately crucial to GM's survival.

Restructuring Boldly: GM shed brands, streamlined operations, and invested in new technologies, setting the stage for a leaner, more future-oriented company.

Wagoner's leadership, though not without controversy and mistakes, exemplifies how a person at the helm of an organization can use the force of a storm to initiate radical changes that might have been impossible during calm weather. The crisis forced GM to innovate, pivot, and emerge more nimble. Like an eagle caught in turbulence, Wagoner had to adapt to the storm's intensity to help elevate the company beyond its status quo.

Parallel to Our Lives: Often, we wait for "the perfect time" to make significant changes. But it's precisely in the storm when we can no longer maintain business as usual that we find the impetus to transform. Our personal storms can prompt us to reevaluate priorities, restructure bad habits, and embrace new disciplines that lead to growth.

Winston Churchill: Rising Above a Nation's Darkest Hour

Few historical figures embody the "eagle mentality" better than Winston Churchill during World War II. When Nazi Germany threatened Britain's survival, Churchill did not cower. Instead, he stirred the nation with a vision that soared above the immediate terror. He famously declared, "We shall fight on the beaches... we shall never surrender," galvanizing an entire people to stand firm.

DON'T CHICKEN OUT, EAGLE IN

Churchill's Eagle Approach

Clarity of Vision: Churchill recognized that moral clarity and national unity could be the wind that lifts Britain out of despair. He never minimized the threat, but he refused to let fear define Britain's future.

Strategic Resilience: He orchestrated alliances (especially with the United States), deployed resources, and used powerful rhetoric to rally the public. Though bombs rained down in the Blitz, Churchill's leadership gave Britain the perspective of eventually overcoming the storm.

Focus on the Higher Purpose: For Churchill, it wasn't just about surviving; it was about preserving democracy, freedom, and the British spirit. That higher purpose often motivates a person (or a nation) to endure hardship and hold onto hope in the darkest times.

Where the average leader might have exhausted all optimism, Churchill saw the storm as a defining trial that could elevate Britain's moral standing and spark global collaboration. This parallels our spiritual walk: the storms we face can either destroy us or refine us, depending on how we respond.

The Biblical Promise: Soaring on Eagles' Wings

The imagery of the eagle in Scripture extends beyond Isaiah 40:3In Exodus 19:4, God says to the Israelites, "I bore you on eagles' wings and brought you to myself," referring to their deliverance from Egypt. The message is clear: God doesn't simply *spare* us from storms; He often *carries* us through them, elevating us beyond what we could have achieved alone.

Why Eagles' Wings?

Strength in Adversity: Eagles have powerful wings capable of carrying them into the fiercest winds. If we trust God, our storms can become sanctuaries of growth rather than cataclysms of defeat.

Divine Assistance: The promise of being carried on eagles' wings suggests we are not alone. While we must still act flap our wings, so to speak God's presence can amplify our efforts.

Perspective Shift: Higher altitude grants a broader view. When life's storms overwhelm us, we can ask God for clarity from above, seeing solutions or insights we missed while grounded in worry.

Our Nigerian friend testified that every time he felt overwhelmed, especially after losing his mother or grappling with finances, prayer and community support offered him a vantage point beyond immediate circumstances. Like an eagle, he was able to look at his situation from a spiritual elevation, discerning paths forward others might have dismissed.

Using the Storm to Propel You

We typically view storms be they emotional, financial, or relational as forces that halt progress. The eagle, by contrast, sees them as wind tunnels to ascend. How can we adopt a similar posture?

Acknowledge the Storm's Reality

Denial traps us at ground level, wasting time and energy. Recognize the crisis for what it is unemployment, betrayal, depression, a floundering business. Acceptance is the first step to leveraging adversity.

Look for the Updraft

Identify aspects of the crisis that can force positive change. For GM, the updraft was the realization that old business models were unsustainable, pushing the company to innovate. For Churchill, the storm of war forced Britain to unify around core values. For you, a personal hardship could spark deeper faith, creativity, or new partnerships.

Spread Your Wings (Take Action)

Don't merely hope the storm passes; actively engage in the process. That could mean seeking counseling, brainstorming new revenue streams, or reconnecting with a long-neglected passion. Like an eagle opening its wings, you must "catch" the opportunities swirling around you.

Maintain Spiritual and Mental Focus

The eagle stays above the turbulence, using strong wings and sharp sight to navigate. We need a disciplined mind, rooted in Scripture and prayer, to remain steady when chaos threatens.

Practical Example: Our Nigerian friend managed to convert repeated moves and financial strain into opportunities. Each transition taught him new entrepreneurial skills (running a poultry business, learning to budget meticulously), which later helped him succeed after moving countries. What started as a series of storms became a series of stepping-stones to personal development.

The Risks of Ground-Level Thinking

If the eagle chooses to remain at ground level during a storm, it risks being battered or drowned by the rain.

DON'T CHICKEN OUT, EAGLE IN

Similarly, we risk stagnation or despair if we *don't* harness adversity for growth. Some common pitfalls of "ground-level thinking" include:

Self-Pity: Feeling perpetually victimized by circumstances, which erodes motivation and creativity.

Anger and Blame: Targeting external factors an unfair boss, a failing economy without considering how we might adapt or respond effectively.

Isolation: Withdrawing from support systems, ignoring the very people who could help us gain new perspective.

Instead, an eagle-minded approach acknowledges difficulty but remains forward-focused. This is exactly what Winston Churchill did: he recognized the dire situation yet continually sought collaboration and reminded Britain that victory was still possible.

Storms as Agents of Transformation

Throughout biblical and modern narratives, storms have a refining effect. They often expose flaws in our foundation whether personal traits like pride, impatience, or poor planning. The automotive crisis exposed GM's inefficiencies. The war tested Britain's resilience. Our personal storms may highlight where we lack discipline, faith, or healthy relationships.

Transformation Steps:

- Identify Structural Weaknesses

Storms can reveal hidden problems, like unresolved trauma or unsustainable debt. Rather than ignoring them, see these revelations as invitations to rebuild stronger.

- Embrace a Teachable Spirit

Humility allows us to learn from adversity. Ask God and trusted mentors, "What are You teaching me in this storm?" Growth demands that we accept lessons we might prefer to dodge.

- Refine or Reorient

Sometimes storms force us to change direction—a new career path, ending a toxic relationship, or reorganizing finances. This can feel scary, but it's akin to the eagle shifting its wings to catch a better gust.

Applying the Eagle Mentality to Everyday Life

It's one thing to be inspired by eagles, Churchill, or corporate turnarounds. But how do we apply these lessons to our day-to-day reality? Let's look at a few common areas:

Career and Business

Identify Growth Opportunities: Instead of seeing layoffs or market downturns solely as threats, consider them catalysts for innovation or upskilling.

Mentorship and Collaboration: Don't fight the storm alone. Seek experienced mentors who've weathered similar gales.

Personal Relationships

Conflict as Catalyst: Relationship storms can force deeper communication and healing if addressed wisely.

Healthy Boundaries: Storms may reveal one-sided relationships; use adversity as a chance to establish healthier dynamics.

Spiritual Journey

Deepened Faith: Storms often dismantle illusions of self-sufficiency. Use challenges as reminders to draw closer to God, practicing prayer and Scripture reading.

Serving Others: Sometimes our personal storms open our eyes to the pain of those around us, prompting empathy and action we never considered before.

Case in Point: During a health crisis, a person might discover an inner resilience previously untapped or realize they must reorganize priorities giving more time to family or philanthropic efforts. While the storm is terrifying, it can elevate them to a more meaningful life perspective.

Testimonies of Soaring

Our Nigerian Friend

Every setback whether academic struggles or cultural transitions eventually strengthened him. Over time, he not only thrived academically but found avenues of entrepreneurship and ministry that might have remained hidden had adversity not pushed him to explore new territories.

Tim Tebow

Repeatedly facing criticism and career uncertainties, Tebow pivoted into philanthropic work and broadcasting. He harnessed public scrutiny to amplify his message of faith, setting up foundations that help children worldwide.

Bethany Hamilton

After losing her arm, she didn't just overcome fear to return to surfing; she also became a beacon of hope for countless people with disabilities. She leveraged her storm to rise above personal tragedy and inspire others.

All these examples share a common thread: adversity wasn't an endpoint, but a launching pad. They *rose* on the back of their storms.

Handling the Fear Factor

A key barrier to adopting the eagle's mindset is fear. Storms are intimidating by nature. It's normal to feel anxious or disoriented. So how do we manage fear without letting it ground us?

Name It: Acknowledge specific worries fear of failure, loss of status, rejection.

Match Fear with Action: Outline concrete steps to mitigate the risk. If you fear financial ruin, create a budget or seek financial advice.

Rehearse God's Faithfulness: Remember past storms you overcame or biblical promises of provision (e.g., Philippians 4:19).

Seek Community Support: Share struggles with trusted friends, mentors, or a support group. Collective wisdom can quell some fears and offer practical solutions.

As Winston Churchill noted, "Fear is a reaction. Courage is a decision." The eagle chooses courage when it spreads its wings against howling winds. We can do likewise when we see storms as an impetus rather than a blockade.

Reflection and Call to Action

Reflect on a current "storm" in your life be it financial strain, a challenging work environment, health concerns, or relational difficulties and clearly articulate it. Then, identify opportunities within this challenge: ask yourself how this adversity might be encouraging growth, adaptation, or innovation, or revealing a divine opportunity.

Commit to taking one bold, actionable step immediately, such as making an important call, seeking new employment, scheduling counseling, or launching a project without waiting for perfect conditions. Regularly ground yourself in prayer and Scripture to maintain a higher perspective, enabling you to rise and navigate your storm with renewed strength.

Moving Forward: Embracing the Next Storm

Storms will come and go throughout our lives. The question is whether we'll remain grounded in fear or adopt the eagle's approach using each storm to propel us

DON'T CHICKEN OUT, EAGLE IN

upward. GM had to restructure to survive. Churchill had to rally a nation to prevent collapse. Our Nigerian friend had to repeatedly adapt for the sake of family and education. The common denominator is not the absence of adversity but the willingness to engage it with trust, creativity, and courage.

Remember Isaiah's promise: those who wait on the Lord renew their strength and soar on wings like eagles. Each storm can build your "wing power," fortifying your faith and honing your vision for the future. Like the eagle, you can rise above the fury of the wind and rain, finding clarity and fresh perspective. The very winds that threaten to tear you down can become the channel that lifts you to unexplored altitudes.

In the following chapters, we will delve more into taking decisive, proactive steps what we've called "taking the bull by the horns." As we shift from the eagle's vantage point of storm-riding to the day-to-day grind of wrestling with challenges, keep in mind that seeing life from above the clouds is part of what gives us the bravery and impetus to charge forward. By combining the eagle's wisdom rising on storms with practical, determined action, we become unstoppable forces for good in our families, communities, and workplaces.

The sky is not just a metaphor for possibility; it's a reminder that there are heights we haven't yet reached perspectives we haven't yet seen. Storms, ironically, might be the key to taking us there. Embrace the winds of adversity, lean on God's unshakeable promise, and prepare to ascend to places you never thought possible. After all, we're not meant to remain huddled in fear on the ground. We're meant to soar.

CHAPTER 7

PURPOSE-DRIVEN PERSEVERANCE

One of the greatest forces in life is the resolve to keep going despite discouragement, setbacks, and lingering doubt. It's what holds you steady when your vision exceeds your present reality, and what draws you forward when easier paths tempt you to give up. While the previous chapters focused on recognizing fear, confronting giants, standing firm, and rising above challenges, this chapter zeroes in on the engine behind enduring success: purpose-driven perseverance.

Why "purpose-driven"? Because perseverance isn't just raw grit or stubborn willpower; it's a pursuit sustained by deeper meaning. When you know *why* you're pushing forward whether it's a calling you believe God placed on your life, a dream to improve your community, or a commitment to your family you find the strength to persist even in the face of overwhelming odds. Purpose transforms obstacles from insurmountable walls into stepping stones, teaching us lessons, refining our character, and ultimately preparing us for the next big leap.

In this chapter, we'll examine how biblical figures and modern heroes alike illustrate the synergy of perseverance and purpose. We'll also look at the story of our Nigerian friend, who managed to turn personal tragedy and financial strain into a platform for entrepreneurial and spiritual growth. By exploring these stories, we'll uncover practical strategies for maintaining a steadfast heart when the road feels impossibly long.

Defining Purpose-Driven Perseverance

Perseverance typically describes the capacity to endure, to keep going in the face of difficulty. It's a quality often praised in everyone from marathon runners to start-up founders. But perseverance alone can sometimes devolve into mere stubbornness or obsession if it lacks a guiding "why."

Purpose is the orienting star that informs *what* we do, *how* we do it, and *why* it matters. When we combine the two perseverance and purpose we get a more sustainable model for pushing through adversity.

Purpose: A guiding sense of mission or calling that frames our goals and sacrifices. In biblical contexts, it often stems from recognizing God's unique calling on our lives.

Perseverance: The unyielding commitment to see something through attending to everyday discipline, sacrifice, and faith even when immediate results are lacking.

A Quick Example

Consider a long-distance runner who trains relentlessly, even in harsh weather. If her sole motivation is *external reward* like winning a medal or social media fame her perseverance may wane if obstacles mount or her fanfare diminishes.

Contrast that with a runner who's running to raise awareness for a cause dear to her heart her ailing parent, or children battling cancer. That deeper purpose can carry her through the darkest days of training because it transcends mere personal gain.

The same applies to our spiritual, relational, and professional endeavors. When your motivation aligns with a calling greater than yourself, perseverance often becomes not just doable, but *inevitable*.

Biblical Foundations: Paul's Race of Endurance

Among biblical examples of purpose-driven perseverance, the Apostle Paul stands out. Once a persecutor of Christians, he had a dramatic encounter with Christ and thereafter lived with an unwavering commitment to spread the gospel. Imprisonments, shipwrecks, beatings, and betrayals became part of his daily reality. Yet Paul's letters reveal a resilient heart that refused to quit.

Key Observations:

Clear Sense of Calling: Paul knew he was called to the Gentiles (Romans 1:1). Purpose gave him direction, telling him which roads to travel and letters to write.

Internal Strength Over Circumstances: Despite hardships being flogged, stoned, and left for dead Paul consistently spoke of "rejoicing in sufferings" because it produced perseverance and character (Romans 5:3-4).

Hope-Filled Perspective: He saw suffering as temporary in light of eternal glory (2 Corinthians 4:17). This eternal viewpoint fueled a relentless pursuit of his mission.

DON'T CHICKEN OUT, EAGLE IN

Paul's life demonstrates how a higher calling can turn setbacks into stepping stones. Rather than concluding that adversity signaled a dead end, he interpreted it as part of the refining process. His purpose overshadowed his fear of pain or rejection.

Modern Illustration: Bethany Hamilton

We've referenced Bethany Hamilton's story before, but it's worth revisiting to showcase purpose-driven perseverance in a modern setting. As a 13-year-old surfer, Bethany lost her arm to a shark attack. Such trauma could easily derail any athletic career. Yet she returned to surfing with an even fiercer drive.

Key Elements of Her Perseverance:

Faith Foundation: She credits her Christian faith as a source of hope and courage.

Identity Beyond Circumstance: Hamilton refused to define herself by the accident. She believed she was called to surf and inspire others, so she pressed on.

Transformation of Adversity into Ministry: Over time, her story became a global testament to overcoming. She authored books, made films, and actively speaks at events using her platform to encourage resilience in others.

Hamilton's perseverance isn't merely physical stamina; it's fueled by a profound sense of purpose faith in God, love for surfing, and the desire to help others find hope. When combined, these factors turned a potentially life-shattering event into a powerful narrative of redemption and perseverance.

The Nigerian Friend: From Heartache to Entrepreneurial Drive

Let's return to our interviewee's journey. Raised as the first of four children, he faced multiple storms: losing his mother during his teenage years, shouldering the family's day-to-day responsibilities, and grappling with financial instability.

Many in his situation might have succumbed to despair or chosen shortcuts to relieve the pressure. But he discovered a sense of purpose in caring for his siblings and pursuing education against all odds.

A Pathway of Purpose and Perseverance

- Early Responsibility

Taking care of siblings built a protective instinct and a genuine desire to see them thrive.

DON'T CHICKEN OUT, EAGLE IN

Despite the weight of chores and academic pressures, he perceived it as a calling: *He was the oldest; it fell on him to ensure the family's well-being.*

- Academic Struggles and Persistence

Math posed a serious hurdle, especially after losing the support of his mother who had been his tutor.

Multiple exam retakes could have discouraged him, but he saw it as a gateway to future opportunities. He viewed the mastery of math not just as a credential but as evidence of his ability to tackle challenges.

- Entrepreneurial Ventures

From poultry farming to a mini gaming shop on campus, he recognized business as a tool to support himself and his siblings.

Each small success further convinced him that he was meant to build and lead something beyond himself, a sense of purpose that bolstered his perseverance.

- Spiritual Anchoring

Active in campus fellowship, he saw his faith as integral, not an optional accessory. He believed God had placed him in these storms to mold his character and expand his impact.

This dual conviction caring for family and serving God infused him with perseverance when obstacles piled high.

Today, looking back, he sees how his purpose shaped his journey. Instead of viewing adversity as punishment, he treated it as preparation for something greater. His story underscores that perseverance isn't mindless slogging; it's persistently moving forward because you believe *there's meaning in each step.*

Purpose Beyond Self: Esther and Daniel Revisited

We've already explored Esther's and Daniel's bold acts Esther in saving her people from genocide, Daniel standing firm in a hostile empire. But consider how *perseverance* played out in their stories:

Esther had to maintain her cover, navigate royal politics, and endure the tension of planning two banquets while the fate of her people hung in the balance. Every day that passed without revealing Haman's plot must have tested her resolve. Yet her purpose to protect her people kept her steady until the right moment.

Daniel displayed a remarkable daily discipline. Praying three times a day, resisting Babylonian assimilation, and serving multiple kings without moral compromise required sustained effort. His ultimate encounter in the lions' den was the culmination of years spent in purposeful faithfulness.

In both accounts, perseverance wasn't a one-time burst of courage; it was an ongoing commitment fueled by a deep sense of calling. That same principle applies to us: we might see a single triumph, but behind it are countless decisions to remain faithful when giving up would seem far easier.

Obstacles to Purpose-Driven Perseverance

Despite the clear benefits of aligning perseverance with purpose, obstacles abound. Recognizing them can help us navigate effectively:

Distraction In a world of endless notifications and competing demands, we can lose sight of our core purpose.

When the "urgent" crowds out the "important," our perseverance falters, as we lack a stable "why" to drive sustained focus.

Immediate Gratification A culture of quick fixes and instant results can undercut long-term commitment.

Purpose-driven goals often yield slow, incremental progress rather than sudden leaps.

Doubt and Discouragement Harsh feedback, repeated failure, or lack of visible progress can erode confidence.

Without an anchor in divine calling or heartfelt convictions, doubt can become a dead end.

Comparison social media and peer successes can tempt us to measure ourselves against others' highlight reels.

This can lead us to question our unique purpose, leading to either envy or a paralyzing sense of inadequacy.

Solution: Each obstacle can be met with a re-centering on purpose: time in prayer, reflection, or conversation with mentors to remind ourselves why we started and for whom we continue.

Spiritual Dimensions of Perseverance

In a biblical worldview, perseverance isn't merely willpower; it's often enabled and empowered by God's grace. James 1:2–4 reminds believers to "count it all joy" when facing trials, recognizing that testing produces perseverance, and perseverance leads to maturity. This spiritual dimension suggests that trials are neither random nor wasted. They're divine tools shaping our character for future works.

DON'T CHICKEN OUT, EAGLE IN

Practical Spiritual Practices

Prayer and Fasting: Like Esther, incorporate periods of focused prayer. When you align your heart with God's perspective, perseverance gains fresh vigor.

Scripture Meditation: Verses like Galatians 6:9 ("Let us not become weary in doing good...") or Hebrews 12:1–2 (running with endurance) can fortify resolve.

Worship and Thanksgiving: Praising God amid trials, as Paul and Silas did in prison, reorients the mind toward hope and possibility.

These disciplines remind us that we're co-laborers with the Lord, not lone warriors slugging it out against cosmic forces. In synergy with divine strength, perseverance transcends mere human determination.

Building the Habit of Perseverance

Purpose-driven perseverance thrives through consistent daily discipline. Begin by setting clear, measurable, and prayerfully discerned goals. Vague ambitions yield half-hearted efforts; specific objectives focus determination, just as our Nigerian friend found clarity in passing exams and supporting his siblings. Next, break large tasks into manageable milestones, celebrating each accomplishment as progress toward fulfillment. Establish accountability through regular check-ins with mentors or supportive peers, reinforcing your motivation and focus. Finally, regularly reflect on your methods, adapting your approach when necessary. Perseverance isn't about blind repetition but about continual growth and thoughtful adjustments.

When Perseverance Seems Impossible: Overcoming "Dark Nights"

Even the most purpose-driven individuals encounter seasons when perseverance feels unattainable. Depression, burnout, or personal crisis can sap energy and cloud vision. In these "dark nights," it's crucial to remember:

Rest Is Not Quitting

Elijah fled to the wilderness, exhausted. God provided food, water, and rest before giving new instructions. Sometimes, the best way to persevere is to pause and recuperate.

Community and Counsel

Seek professional help if you battle severe depression or anxiety. Purpose-driven perseverance doesn't exclude therapy or pastoral counseling; these can be God's instruments for restoration.

DON'T CHICKEN OUT, EAGLE IN

Focus on the Next Step

Instead of fretting over the entire journey, zero in on immediate tasks like finishing today's assignment or reaching out to a supportive friend.

Recall Past Victories

Keeping a journal of answered prayers and past breakthroughs can reignite hope. Our interviewee kept track of small entrepreneurial wins to remind himself that obstacles can indeed be overcome.

The Ripple Effect of Perseverance

Perseverance rarely benefits just one person. Others witness your commitment and are encouraged to push through their own battles. This ripple effect appears in each of our biblical and modern examples:

Paul turned the hardships of imprisonment into letters that still nourish the Church centuries later.

Bethany Hamilton inspires countless individuals facing physical challenges, proof that life doesn't end with tragedy.

Esther and Daniel lifted entire nations by refusing to abandon their posts.

Our Nigerian friend's younger siblings learned to value faith, hard work, and resilience by watching him juggle multiple responsibilities. Some have gone on to follow in his footsteps, fostering their own entrepreneurial dreams or volunteering in church communities.

When we persevere with purpose, we effectively carve pathways for others to follow. Your steadfast example might be exactly what a struggling friend, neighbor, or coworker needs to see.

Practical Examples of Purpose-Driven Perseverance

Corporate World

David Green (Hobby Lobby): Stayed true to his Christian convictions despite immense pressure, eventually winning a significant Supreme Court case related to corporate policies and religious beliefs. Perseverance in upholding moral standards shaped corporate culture and influenced public discourse.

Ministry and Church Life

Chad Veach (Zoe Church): Leading a church in a city as high-powered as Los Angeles is no small feat, especially when biblical principles conflict with mainstream culture. Consistent, purposeful preaching and compassionate community outreach have expanded

DON'T CHICKEN OUT, EAGLE IN

Zoe Church's impact. Veach's perseverance stems from a clear conviction that L.A. needs authentic spiritual transformation.

Personal Challenges

A single [arent might endure financial hardships, hectic schedules, and limited personal time, yet remain steadfast in raising children with love and discipline. Their sense of *why* the children's future drives them beyond exhaustion.

A student with learning disabilities might press through repeated failures, buoyed by a conviction that success in a chosen field matters not just for a diploma but for building confidence and potential testimonies that will help others in similar situations.

In each scenario, purpose fuels the engine of perseverance, transforming everyday struggles into stories of triumph.

Reflection and Next Steps

By now, you've seen that purpose-driven perseverance is more than a motivational slogan. It's the day-to-day expression of a life anchored in deep conviction, guided by faith, and sustained by hope for something greater than instant gratification. As we close this chapter, consider these steps:

Identify Your Core Purpose Spend time in prayer, journaling, or discussing with mentors to clarify what truly drives you. Is it a sense of divine calling? A passion for justice? A desire to provide for family?

Set Immediate and Long-Term Goals Break down your overarching purpose into tangible milestones. Don't just say, "I want to help the community." Define *how* through volunteering, specific advocacy, or philanthropic efforts.

Establish Support Systems Build a network of people who share or respect your purpose family, friends, church groups, or professional mentors. Let them encourage you and be open about your challenges.

Regularly Revisit Your "Why" Life is noisy, and it's easy to get off track. Schedule periodic reviews maybe weekly or monthly to ask, "Am I still aligned with my purpose?"

Celebrate Progress, Not Just Outcomes Perseverance is a marathon. Small wins along the way like completing a course, saving a bit of money, reconciling a conflict are worthy of acknowledgment and gratitude.

DON'T CHICKEN OUT, EAGLE IN

Parting Thought: James 1:4 says, "Let perseverance finish its work so that you may be mature and complete, not lacking anything." Notice that perseverance has a "work" to do in us. It refines, matures, and readies us for the larger tasks and blessings ahead.

Without perseverance, we stay half-formed, easily dismayed by failure. With it, we become vessels through which divine purpose flows, blessing both our own lives and the world around us.

Conclusion: Embrace the Long Game

Purpose-driven perseverance isn't glamorous moment by moment. It looks like studying late at night, going the extra mile at work, praying when results are invisible, and acting with integrity when shortcuts beckon. But as each of our stories from ancient Israel to modern Nigeria illustrates, it's these very disciplines that lead to breakthroughs, transformations, and legacies of hope.

The question is not whether adversity will arise it will. Nor is it whether you'll feel tempted to abandon your post most people do at some point. Rather, the question is whether you'll keep your eye on the deeper mission God has instilled in your heart. If the answer is yes, then your perseverance transcends mere endurance; it becomes a powerful, divinely inspired force for shaping your destiny and uplifting others in the process.

Let this chapter serve as a reminder and challenge: your purpose is bigger than your pain, and your destiny more enduring than your disappointments. Keep running, keep building, keep praying. Each step matters.

In the subsequent chapters, we'll continue exploring how to turn adversity into traction as we move ever closer to the fearless, eagle-like existence we were created to live. So hold tight to your purpose and let perseverance guide you into the life you've only glimpsed in your most hopeful moments.

You are, after all, on a journey not just to survive but to soar.

CHAPTER 8

CULTIVATING RESILIENCE THROUGH COMMUNITY

Resilience isn't formed in isolation; it's a communal process. Think of a young plant in a garden: even the most robust seed needs sunlight, water, nutrients, and an ecosystem that supports growth. In the same way, resilience the capacity to bounce back from adversity thrives best in the fertile soil of community. While personal resolve matters, individuals often discover that their greatest breakthroughs occur when they find allies, mentors, and encouragers who stand with them in life's storms.

In the previous chapters, we explored how fear can masquerade as caution, how biblical heroes rose against formidable odds, and how perseverance rooted in purpose can transform trials into triumphs. Now, Chapter 8 focuses on a crucial dimension of the "Eagle In" life: the synergy of resilience and community. Our biblical narratives David, Daniel, Esther illustrate that no one thrives alone. Even eagles eventually teach their young to fly and, at times, will even carry them. As we will see, modern examples and our Nigerian friend's journey also remind us that strong support networks can magnify our faith, courage, and ability to endure.

The Myth of the Lone Hero

Our culture often exalts the solitary hero archetype the rugged individual who conquers challenges alone and emerges victorious. Movies, novels, and sometimes even sermons can overemphasize personal grit without acknowledging the reality that victories are often collective efforts.

David had Jonathan, whose friendship and loyalty bolstered him during King Saul's hostility.

Daniel wasn't the only devout Jew in Babylon; his friends Shadrach, Meshach, and Abednego also refused to compromise. Their shared commitment fortified Daniel's faith.

DON'T CHICKEN OUT, EAGLE IN

Esther didn't act alone to save her people; she relied on Mordecai's guidance and the communal fasting of the Jewish community.

This underscores a crucial lesson: *individual brilliance flourishes in a framework of communal support.* The notion that you must or can do it all on your own is largely a myth, and it often leads to isolation, burnout, and missed potential.

Biblical Example: The Power of Together

The Scriptures overflow with examples of how faith and resilience grow within a network of believers:

Moses, Aaron, and Hur (Exodus 17): In the battle against the Amalekites, Moses stood on a hill with his arms raised. When his arms grew weary and started to fall, the Israelites began losing ground. Aaron and Hur stepped in to hold up Moses' arms, ensuring victory. Without them, Moses' physical limitations would have spelled defeat.

The Early Church (Acts 2:42–47): After Pentecost, believers gathered daily, sharing resources and supporting one another in prayer and fellowship. This sense of unity wasn't just a feel-good story; it was vital for surviving persecution and spreading the gospel.

Paul's Collaborators: Though Paul is often seen as a lone missionary force, he routinely acknowledged co-laborers like Barnabas, Silas, Timothy, and Priscilla and Aquila, whose partnership advanced the mission significantly.

In every case, communal ties magnified individual callings. They also modeled how practical support holding someone's arms up or sharing food can be as impactful as spiritual encouragement.

Why Resilience Needs Community

Resilience the ability to recover quickly from difficulties is often seen as a personal trait built on optimism, self-discipline, and problem-solving skills. Yet community profoundly enhances and accelerates resilience in ways that personal effort alone cannot.

One key benefit is emotional support. As social beings, we find that emotional burdens become lighter when shared. A compassionate community offers empathy, reminding us that we are not alone in our struggles.

Community also fosters resource sharing. A supportive network can step in with practical help whether financial assistance, job referrals, skill mentorship, or childcare support. These resources can ease immediate pressures, freeing individuals to focus on solving deeper, long-term challenges.

Additionally, community provides accountability and motivation. Sharing goals within a group setting naturally strengthens follow-through. Knowing that others are praying for you, awaiting updates, or depending on your participation fuels discipline and perseverance in powerful ways.

Modern examples abound. Support groups for addiction recovery, business mastermind groups for entrepreneurs, and home groups in churches all illustrate how the synergy of collective wisdom and encouragement can empower individuals to press on when they might otherwise have quit.

Our Nigerian Friend's Experience: Community at Work

Throughout these pages, we've noted how our Nigerian friend navigated multiple storms financial hardship, academic hurdles, and the loss of a parent. But it wasn't sheer willpower alone that carried him; community played a significant role:

Family Ties: Even as the firstborn, he wasn't solely responsible for his siblings. Extended relatives, church members, and family friends helped with advice, occasional loans, or shared childcare duties.

Campus Fellowship: Participating in a campus Christian fellowship offered spiritual nourishment and social bonds. He found mentors there who guided him academically and spiritually, shaping his leadership skills.

Entrepreneurial Allies: While running small businesses like a poultry farm and a mini gaming shop, he sought out peers who were also trying to make ends meet. They exchanged tips, introduced each other to buyers, and formed small networks of mutual benefit.

Reflecting on his journey, he attributes at least half of his success to community support. In times of doubt, prayer partners in fellowship reminded him of God's promises. When finances ran dry, friends offered microloans or shared "inside tips" on better poultry feed or gaming business strategies. Community didn't spare him from storms, but it kept him afloat when he might have otherwise sunk.

Finding or Building Your Community

Not everyone starts life with a built-in support network. Some come from fractured families or lead lives marked by frequent moves, making community formation a real challenge. If that's your situation, take heart community can be cultivated intentionally.

The first step is to initiate connection. Waiting passively seldom works. Attend local churches, community centers, or volunteer programs. Introduce yourself, start conversations, and join group activities that align with your interests or faith.

Joining small groups or home fellowships is another effective strategy. In many churches, smaller gatherings offer richer opportunities for prayer, discussion, and friendship than large Sunday services. If local options are scarce, online forums or interest-based groups can be a good starting point.

It's also powerful to offer what you have. Friendships often form when you serve others or share your skills. Baking for a church event, teaching a class, or mentoring a student can lead to organic relationships built on trust and reciprocity.

Finally, stay vulnerable and authentic. True community forms not through perfection, but through shared struggles and victories. By letting go of the need to project an image of having it all together, you invite others into a space of empathy and mutual support.

Biblical Note: Even Jesus had a "community" the Twelve disciples. He taught them, ate with them, and prayed with them. They, in turn, learned to depend on one another. If the Son of God didn't attempt a lone-wolf approach, we likely shouldn't either.

Nurturing Healthy Community Dynamics

Community is a double-edged sword: it can uplift and strengthen, or, if unhealthy, drag us into negativity. That's why cultivating healthy dynamics is essential for any life-giving community.

At the core of a healthy community are shared values. While total agreement on every detail isn't necessary, a common faith or purpose forms a strong foundation that keeps the group united even through disagreements.

Equally important is mutual respect. True community makes space for candid conversations where members feel safe to speak openly without fear of ridicule. Genuine accountability happens when people can both correct and encourage one another with gentleness.

Conflict resolution is inevitable in any group, but what distinguishes a thriving community is the willingness to address disagreements head-on. Listening actively, apologizing sincerely, and seeking common ground ensures that conflicts refine rather than fracture relationships.

A truly resilient community also builds an encouragement culture. While it's easy to critique, a healthy group makes a habit of noticing progress, celebrating small wins, and speaking life into one another's journeys.

The biblical example of Barnabas captures this beautifully. His name, meaning "son of encouragement," reflected his actions: he vouched for Paul when others doubted his conversion, traveled with him on mission journeys, and later mentored John Mark after Paul had given up on him. Barnabas embodied the power of a positive, affirming presence fostering ministries and lives simply by believing in others.

Corporate or Professional Communities

Resilience through community isn't limited to religious or social circles. In a business or professional context:

Mastermind Groups: Entrepreneurs gather regularly to share challenges, brainstorm solutions, and hold each other accountable. Many credit these small groups with fueling exponential growth in their ventures.

Mentorship Networks: Young professionals who connect with mentors often navigate career storms better. A mentor offers perspective, warns of pitfalls, and may open doors otherwise closed.

Team Culture: A healthy team extends beyond job titles, supporting each other during tight deadlines or personal crises. Think of Winston Churchill rallying Britain or Rick Wagoner steering GM success was never a solo endeavor; it took cohesive teams.

In each scenario, the principle remains: *we multiply our resilience when we engage with others who share our burdens and help chart the path forward.*

The Spiritual Practice of Bearing One Another's Burdens

The New Testament calls believers to "bear one another's burdens" (Galatians 6:2), reminding us that this is not an optional courtesy but a central practice of Christian community. It's a sacred act that takes many forms.

One way we fulfill this calling is through prayer partnerships. Knowing that someone is consistently interceding for you infuses fresh courage and deepens the bond of fellowship. Prayer weaves our lives together, knitting a network of mutual care and spiritual intimacy.

DON'T CHICKEN OUT, EAGLE IN

Practical acts of service also embody this command. Cooking for a sick friend, offering to babysit for a single parent, or pooling resources to cover a community member's unexpected bills are tangible expressions of Christ's love. These small, concrete actions build resilience and trust within the body.

Equally important is offering emotional and spiritual support. Sometimes the greatest gift we can give is simply our presence listening, weeping together, rejoicing together. In these moments, we help each other carry loads too heavy to bear alone.

True burden bearing fosters a community where vulnerability is not seen as weakness, and asking for help is not a sign of failure. Instead, it reveals the truth that we are better together than we ever could be alone.

Overcoming Relational Barriers to Community

Forming or joining a supportive network can be challenging, especially if you've faced betrayals, rejections, or personal anxieties. Several common barriers often stand in the way.

One is the fear of judgment. Past experiences of being mocked or misunderstood can cause people to hide their struggles. However, a loving community demonstrates empathy and patience. Sharing your story in small increments can gradually build the trust needed for deeper connection.

Another barrier stems from cultural norms of independence. In some backgrounds, self-reliance is highly prized, and asking for help feels shameful. Yet Scripture and countless testimonies remind us that life is meant to be lived in shared burdens, not solitary battles.

Introversion or social anxiety can also make community feel overwhelming. In these cases, smaller group settings or one-on-one meetups can provide a more manageable path to building relationships organically and comfortably.

Finally, time constraints are a real obstacle. Busy schedules leave little margin for community-building. Yet even small investments of intentional time a weekly coffee with a friend, a quick prayer call can yield exponential benefits in resilience and support.

Action Step: If any of these barriers resonate with you, choose one or two small, practical steps—such as attending a local meetup or texting a potential mentor to begin moving toward deeper engagement. Small beginnings can lead to lasting community.

DON'T CHICKEN OUT, EAGLE IN

Harnessing Technology Wisely

The digital age presents both immense opportunities and pitfalls for community:

Opportunity: Online platforms Zoom prayer meetings, WhatsApp Bible studies, Facebook groups can unite believers across geographies. Our Nigerian friend, after moving to the U.S., stayed connected with his home fellowship via social media, receiving ongoing encouragement.

Pitfall: Not all online spaces are healthy. Social media can also breed superficial interactions, envy, or toxic debates. It's crucial to discern which digital forums genuinely enrich your faith and resilience.

When used wisely, technology can extend your support network beyond local boundaries. But it never replaces in-person fellowship. A balanced approach harnesses online tools while still prioritizing real-life connections.

The Collective Impact: More Than an Individual Gain

Building a resilient community isn't just about personal benefit it creates a ripple effect that extends far beyond ourselves. When you invest in others' growth and they invest in you, entire groups, churches, and even cities can flourish.

For example, church revivals often spring from congregations that pray and serve together. Their unity births renewal movements that feed the hungry, mentor the next generation, and plant new ministries that impact entire regions.

Similarly, small business ecosystems thrive when local entrepreneurs support one another. Through collaboration and encouragement, they create vibrant business districts, generate employment, and foster shared prosperity.

In families, the impact can be just as profound. Family legacies built around faith and mutual support can shift generational outcomes reducing financial struggles, strengthening moral foundations, and passing on resilience to future generations.

This bigger-picture view reminds us that resilience, when nurtured in community, becomes a kingdom-level force. As you strengthen your personal endurance, you're not just securing your own future you're becoming part of a living tapestry that blesses countless others far beyond your immediate circle.

DON'T CHICKEN OUT, EAGLE IN

Reflection: Embracing God's Design for Togetherness

From the very beginning when God declared, "It is not good for man to be alone" to the New Testament's imagery of the Body of Christ, Scripture consistently portrays human beings as deeply interdependent. Embracing the "Eagle In" mindset means recognizing this divine design: we are meant to lean on each other.

A practical first step is to audit your current networks. Reflect on whom you rely on spiritually, emotionally, and practically and consider whom you are supporting in return. Identifying gaps can guide you toward intentional growth in community.

Next, pray for divine appointments. Ask God to bring mentors, peers, and partners who can challenge, encourage, and journey with you. Stay open, because often these connections emerge in unexpected places.

Approaching relationships with a service mindset is also crucial. Rather than waiting to be blessed, seek ways to bless others first. Many of the strongest bonds are forged when we help meet someone else's need and, in doing so, find mutual support.

Consistency matters too. Whether it's a weekly small group, a monthly mastermind, or a daily phone call, regular gatherings foster the deeper bonds that sustain us through life's storms.

Finally, cultivate gratitude. Thank God for the people He places in your life and take time to express appreciation to those who walk with you. Gratitude strengthens existing relationships and invites even more blessings.

Closing Thought

Resilience through community is not a backup plan it's an integral part of God's blueprint for human flourishing. A single eagle can soar magnificently, but even eagles gather at key points in their journey young ones needing guidance, elders teaching how to harness the wind. You were not designed to face storms alone. Embracing community doesn't weaken your independence; it elevates your ability to endure, innovate, and ultimately triumph.

As we move into the next chapters, we'll explore how to take bold action "taking the bull by the horns"—and deepen our trust in God's strength through storms. But remember this: behind every fearless step you take, a community is cheering you on, holding you accountable, and celebrating your victories. Together, we soar higher than we ever could alone.

CHAPTER 9

NAVIGATING TRANSITIONS:

LEAPS OF FAITH IN CAREER AND LIFE

Life inevitably brings transitions new jobs, relocations, shifting relationships, or entire career pivots. Sometimes these changes come by choice; other times, they're thrust upon us. Either way, such transitions can shake our sense of identity and security, leaving us standing at a crossroads where fear and faith converge. It's at this juncture that we often face a defining question: Will I take a leap of faith into the unknown, or remain anchored in what's safe and familiar?

In previous chapters, we explored how characters like David, Daniel, and Esther confronted adversity with courage, how the eagle uses storms to ascend, and how resilience grows best within communities.

Now, in Chapter 9, we turn specifically to those *liminal* moments times when one season is ending and another is beginning. Like Abraham leaving his homeland or our Nigerian friend relocating to a new country, these leaps of faith can become spiritual catalysts, refining our trust in God and shaping our destiny. Through biblical narratives, modern examples, and tangible advice, we'll learn strategies for navigating transitions without succumbing to fear.

The Nature of Transition: Risk and Opportunity

Transitions, by nature, are filled with uncertainty. While they can stir excitement about fresh possibilities, they also threaten our comfort zones. A new career path might mean leaving behind familiar colleagues. A relocation could force us to rebuild social networks from scratch. Even positive changes, such as marriage or the birth of a child, challenge the routines we once found predictable.

Yet transitions are not merely disruptions; they are opportunities in disguise. They catalyze growth by removing old structures, pushing us to develop new skills, adopt fresh mindsets, and form new relationships.

DON'T CHICKEN OUT, EAGLE IN

They deepen faith, nudging us to depend more fully on God when we feel out of our depth. And they clarify purpose, as stepping away from familiar environments often reveals what we truly value.

Navigating transitions, then, is less about avoiding discomfort and more about harnessing the hidden potential in each new chapter.

Biblical Foundations: Abraham's Leap into the Unknown

A quintessential biblical illustration of transition is the story of Abraham (then Abram). In Genesis 12, God tells him, "Go from your country, your people and your father's household to the land I will show you." Abraham wasn't handed a detailed map or a clear timeline. What he received was a promise that through him, "all peoples on earth will be blessed."

Abraham's journey teaches us that obedience often precedes clarity. He had to act on God's call without knowing exactly where he was going. Similarly, many of our transitions require us to move forward before all the pieces are in place.

His story also reminds us that risk, when covered by divine promise, is not reckless. From a human perspective, Abraham risked his family's safety and his own reputation. Yet God's assurance underscored that he was not stepping into the unknown alone.

Finally, Abraham's leap of faith had a legacy impact. His obedience became the foundation for blessings that rippled through countless generations. In the same way, our willingness to trust God through transitions can open doors of blessing not only for ourselves but for those who follow.

Abraham's narrative resonates deeply today. Transitions still demand partial "blindness." We often sense God's tug toward a new direction a career shift, a ministry endeavor, a physical move without knowing all the details. Yet the invitation remains the same: step forward in trust, believing that God will unfold the path as we move.

Leaps in Career: When to Pivot

In today's world, career transitions are common. Some are minor, like shifting roles within the same company. Others are more dramatic leaving behind a stable profession to pursue a passion project or a philanthropic mission. Navigating these moments requires careful discernment.

It often begins with identifying the nudge. Feelings of restlessness or discontent might be signs that God is prompting a change. However, not every restless urge is divine. Prayer, heart-checks, and wise counsel are crucial for discerning whether a shift is truly Spirit-led.

Once the prompting is clear, it's important to count the cost. Jesus taught the wisdom of calculating costs (Luke 14:28). A career leap might mean a temporary reduction in income, additional training, or a slower path to stability. Being realistic about these factors doesn't weaken our faith it strengthens wise planning.

Before taking a giant leap, it's often wise to test the waters. Starting a side hustle, volunteering, or engaging part-time in the new field can build both confidence and practical experience. It allows you to gather insight without risking everything at once.

Through it all, we must trust in divine provision. Career transitions naturally provoke anxiety about finances and future stability. Yet the story of Israel's daily manna reminds us that while strategic planning matters, our ultimate security rests in a faithful God who can open doors we never anticipated.

Case in Point

A teacher who feels an increasing call to missions might begin by volunteering during summer breaks, participating in short-term trips, or obtaining certification in cross-cultural ministry. These small steps of faith allow for discernment before making a final, life-altering decision.

Life Transitions and Identity Shifts

Not every major transition revolves around work. Some of the most profound shifts are deeply personal and require us to reconsider our very identity.

Marriage, for instance, redefines daily rhythms, finances, and emotional energy. Conversely, entering a season of singleness whether by choice, divorce, or widowhood brings its own emotional and spiritual recalibrations.

Parenthood dramatically alters priorities, sleep schedules, and even one's sense of self. Similarly, retirement, while often celebrated as freedom, can trigger an identity crisis after decades spent defining oneself through work.

Then there's the transition of caring for aging parents. Balancing your own career and personal life with a caregiving role can introduce emotional, logistical, and spiritual complexities you may never have anticipated.

DON'T CHICKEN OUT, EAGLE IN

Each of these scenarios forces us to pause and ask: Who am I now? and How does my faith shape my new role? Recognizing that transitions naturally reshape identity helps us extend patience and grace to ourselves. Letting go of an old season can be just as challenging and just as holy as stepping into a new one.

Our Nigerian Friend's Major Leap: Emigrating to the U.S.

We've seen this friend's story woven throughout previous chapters how he managed finances for his family, overcame academic struggles, and built small entrepreneurial ventures. His transition from Nigeria to the United States stands as one of his most defining leaps of faith.

During the preparation stage, he spent countless hours researching universities and job opportunities, while praying fervently for clarity. At the same time, he saved diligently, balancing entrepreneurial efforts with family obligations, knowing the move would demand significant resources.

When the moment came, tearing away from comfort proved deeply painful. Leaving behind siblings, extended family, and a beloved church fellowship was no small sacrifice. Emotional ties made the decision heart-wrenching, casting a long shadow of homesickness even before he boarded the plane.

The initial challenges in the U.S. tested his resolve daily. Culture shock, unfamiliar accents, different social norms, and occasional experiences of discrimination made him question whether he had made the right choice. Some days, despair loomed large.

Yet community support became a lifeline. Local church members, diaspora communities, and a few university peers formed a safety net helping him secure housing, navigate complicated paperwork, and even connecting him with job opportunities. Their kindness reminded him that God had not abandoned him to walk this new path alone.

In time, new opportunities blossomed. He furthered his education, sharpened his business skills, and developed a ministry that bridged Nigerian and American cultural contexts. This beautiful alignment of faith and career might never have flourished had he not taken that leap into the unknown.

His testimony stands as a vivid reminder: transitions can feel overwhelming and fraught with loss, but for those willing to trust God amid uncertainties, the blessings can far outweigh the initial distress.

DON'T CHICKEN OUT, EAGLE IN

Strategies for Navigating Transitions with Grace

Navigating transitions with grace calls for a blend of spiritual attentiveness and practical wisdom.

The journey begins with spiritual discernment. Prayer, fasting, and seeking wise counsel from trusted mentors or pastors can prevent rash decisions. Like Esther, who called for a season of focused prayer before risking her life for her people, we too can pause and seek divine guidance before making major moves.

Alongside spiritual preparation comes practical planning. Doing your research, creating realistic budgets, and exploring your prospective environment are crucial steps. While Abraham journeyed without a detailed map, he still traveled known caravan routes and brought essential supplies. Faith and preparation work hand in hand.

Adopting a "settling in" mindset is also key. Rather than viewing a new season as purely experimental, invest yourself fully. In Jeremiah 29:5–7, the exiled Israelites were instructed to build houses, plant gardens, and seek the prosperity of the city where they lived even as exiles, they were called to put down roots. A committed attitude fosters deeper growth.

Continuous evaluation helps you stay adaptable. Once you've entered the new environment, remain sensitive to the Spirit's leading. Sometimes the "promised land" doesn't look as expected. Like Paul's missionary journeys, a closed door in one place may redirect you to unexpected opportunities elsewhere.

Finally, it's vital to leverage community. Resist the temptation to navigate transition alone. Whether relocating for work or stepping into marriage, rally supportive friends, family, or church members around you. Even virtual groups can provide lifelines of encouragement when geographical distance poses challenges.

The Emotional Roller Coaster of Transition

Transitions naturally bring a swirl of emotions, and it's important to recognize and honor them rather than suppress or deny them.

At the outset, excitement often fills the air. New horizons can feel like a grand adventure, full of hope and possibilities.

Soon after, anxiety may creep in as reality sets in financial pressures, relational tensions, or cultural adjustments that weren't anticipated.

DON'T CHICKEN OUT, EAGLE IN

There may also be seasons of loneliness or nostalgia for the old life, especially when facing challenges that highlight everything unfamiliar or difficult about the new situation.

Over time, however, gradual adaptation unfolds. New routines and friendships begin to form, and small glimpses of God's hand at work become evident, shaping the future in ways you hadn't imagined.

Allowing these emotions the space to be felt and resisting the urge to judge yourself harshly for experiencing them eases the strain. Journaling your journey, seeking out conversations with a spiritual mentor, or simply praying honestly about each emotional wave can help anchor your faith and steady your heart in the midst of the storm.

Modern Parallels and Success Stories

Transitions are not just ancient or biblical realities they're woven into modern life as well, often shaping the very fabric of industries, ministries, and personal journeys.

In the corporate world, Rick Wagoner, the CEO of General Motors during the 2008 financial crisis, faced a transition no one wanted. Leading a massive restructuring during a period of economic collapse was gruelling, but it ultimately pushed GM into adopting new strategies and technologies. Though painful, the transition preserved and revitalized an iconic company.

Meanwhile, in ministry, Chad Veach has exemplified the power of navigating cultural shifts with grace. Pastoring a church in Los Angeles a city known for entertainment, diversity, and a general skepticism toward traditional faith he blended biblical teaching with cultural sensitivity. The result is a thriving faith community that resonates with people who might have otherwise remained uninterested in church life.

On a more personal level, Bethany Hamilton's story highlights how unexpected transitions can lead to broader impact. After losing her arm in a shark attack, she transitioned from being simply a competitive surfer to becoming an inspirational figure around the world. Through speaking engagements, media appearances, and new relationships, Bethany stepped outside her comfort zone to touch countless lives.

Each of these examples echoes a deep principle: transitions especially unwanted or unexpected ones can foster extraordinary innovation and deeper impact. While the cost often includes anxiety, self-doubt, and the risk of failure, the payoff can redefine industries, ministries, and personal legacies.

DON'T CHICKEN OUT, EAGLE IN

Spiritual Anchor: Trust in God's Guidance

At the heart of navigating transitions is not simply mental toughness or flawless planning. It is a profound trust that God remains faithful to lead us through every unknown.

Biblical history reminds us of this pattern again and again. Israel's Exodus was a momentous transition from slavery to freedom. Despite frequent grumbling and moments of idolatry, God's presence symbolized by pillars of cloud and fire never wavered.

Similarly, Ruth and Naomi, after losing their husbands, journeyed from Moab back to Bethlehem. In their grief, they clung to each other and to God's covenant promises. Their faithfulness during transition positioned them within the lineage of King David and ultimately, Jesus Himself.

The Apostle Paul's missionary journeys offer another powerful example. Shipwrecked, imprisoned, and often facing fierce opposition, Paul pressed forward, trusting that the same God who guided him yesterday would guide him into each new city and mission field.

The application is clear: regular prayer, deep reflection on Scripture, and reminders of God's past faithfulness both biblical and personal infuse us with courage to take the next step. Our anchor is not in the certainty of circumstances but in the unchanging character of God, who orchestrates each season of our lives for His glory and our ultimate good.

Overcoming Fear in the "In-Between"

The in-between the space between letting go of the old and fully settling into the new can feel especially nerve-racking. Fear often intensifies in this season, whispering that we've made the wrong decision, or that failure is inevitable.

One powerful first step is to name the fear. Concretely identifying what you are afraid of whether it's financial ruin, loneliness, embarrassment, or something else helps disarm the vague, paralyzing anxiety that thrives in the shadows. Naming it brings it into the light.

Next, it's crucial to counter fear with truth. Draw strength from Scripture and from personal testimonies. If finances are your worry, remember how God provided for Elijah through ravens, or multiplied the oil for a widow. If loneliness feels overwhelming, cling to the promise that God places the lonely in families (Psalm 68:6).

Taking micro steps can also ease the overwhelm. Often, it's the enormity of the whole journey that intimidates us. Breaking your transition into smaller, manageable tasks or goals helps maintain momentum and builds confidence along the way.

And remember to lean on support systems. As discussed earlier, community is vital. Sharing your fears with prayer partners, mentors, or trusted friends ensures you are not battling inner anxieties alone. Their encouragement, prayers, and wisdom can be lifelines when your courage wavers.

Ultimately, fear, though uncomfortable, can become a catalyst for transformation. Every time we push through it, we strengthen spiritual muscles, preparing ourselves for even bigger leaps of faith ahead. Fear is not a signal to retreat it's often a doorway to deeper growth.

Embracing Divine Surprises

Transitions often usher in divine surprises opportunities and blessings we could never have predicted. Abraham likely never imagined he would father a son at the age of 100 or become the ancestor of nations. Similarly, our Nigerian friend initially sought a better life, but along the way discovered a ministry calling that merged his cross-cultural experiences into something far beyond his original dreams.

Your leap of faith might reveal new talents, unexpected relationships, or open doors you couldn't have envisioned while standing in your old environment.

To embrace these divine surprises, wait expectantly. Faith includes being ready for God's "bigger than expected" answers. Stay flexible, allowing room for the journey to diverge from your initial plan if divine confirmation resonates. And cultivate gratitude along the way. Even small surprises an unexpected friendship, a minor open door deserve celebration. Gratitude keeps your heart postured to receive even more.

Conclusion: Step Forward, Rooted in Faith

Transitions are rarely straightforward. They stretch and test our trust, resilience, and adaptability. Yet each leap of faith whether changing careers, moving countries, entering a new family role, or stepping into leadership can become a milestone in our spiritual journey.

Identity shifts, homesickness, and fears of failure are real, but Scripture and modern testimonies alike echo a timeless truth: God's presence remains steadfast, and His grace is sufficient for every new chapter.

As you reflect, consider a few practical steps:

DON'T CHICKEN OUT, EAGLE IN

- ☐ Revisit your motivations. Are you pursuing this transition out of fear, pressure, or truly sensing God's leading? A clear "why" can sustain you through the difficult moments.

- ☐ Plan responsibly but trust completely. Seek wise counsel, do your research, and count the costs yet hold your plans loosely, acknowledging that God's sovereignty reigns above all.

- ☐ Seek support. Don't walk alone. Lean into your church, small group, or trusted friends who can pray, encourage, and offer practical help when needed.

- ☐ Celebrate milestones. Whether it's finding an apartment, completing a training, or surviving the first challenging week, mark these victories. Celebrating fosters endurance and joy.

- ☐ Pray for guidance daily. Commit your anxieties, decisions, and celebrations to God. Trust that, as Proverbs 3:5–6 promises, He will direct your paths.

Transitions are less about moving from one place to another, and more about the transformation God accomplishes along the way. Like an eagle that spreads its wings in the midst of a storm, you, too, can harness the winds of change to rise to new spiritual and personal heights.

Abraham's simple obedience his willingness to step into the unknown set a course that blessed innumerable generations. Your leap of faith, anchored in God's wisdom and guided by humility, might similarly reshape your life in ways you cannot yet see.

So, step forward. The next season may be unknown, but the One who calls you is faithful. Even if the path ahead is hidden, trust the voice that leads you, one step at a time.

Let this be your prayer:

"Lord, I am ready to leap, trusting that You will catch me, guide me, and use me for something greater than I dare to imagine."

Embrace the transition. It may just be the threshold to your greatest growth.

DON'T CHICKEN OUT, EAGLE IN

CHAPTER 10

TAKE THE BULL BY THE HORN

THE POWER OF DECISIVE ACTION

In any journey of faith and personal growth, there comes a moment when reflection, planning, and intention must give way to bold, decisive action. You can understand fear intimately, cultivate resilience in community, and explore your options with great care but if you never actually step onto the battlefield, you will never taste the victory. This is the essence of "taking the bull by the horn": facing the challenge head-on, harnessing your God-given agency, and transforming intention into progress.

Throughout the chapters so far, we've explored how biblical figures overcame giants, lion's dens, and impossible odds; how modern individuals harness storms to ascend; and how transitions can become catalysts for a deeper walk with God.

Now, in Chapter 10, we turn our focus to the act of taking bold steps closing the gap between what you know and what you do. If fear is a tether that keeps you grounded, then decisive action is the break in the chain, propelling you into new territory. We'll explore why action matters, how to overcome common barriers, and what it looks like to move beyond theory into the realm of tangible breakthroughs.

Why Action Matters

Many people stay stuck for years not because they lack knowledge or resources, but because they never take the leap. They accumulate information, read books, watch motivational videos, or even pray fervently yet avoid making real moves. Jesus captured this in the parable of the two sons (Matthew 21:28–31).

One son says he will do the work but doesn't; the other initially refuses but eventually acts. Jesus commended the one who followed through, underscoring that obedience in action reflects genuine commitment more than words or good intentions ever can.

DON'T CHICKEN OUT, EAGLE IN

The danger of endless preparation is real. Analysis paralysis continually seeking the "perfect time" or "perfect plan" can morph into perpetual hesitation. Each day of inaction erodes confidence; humans are wired to find motivation in progress, and stagnation saps morale.

Spiritually, James 2:17 reminds us that faith without works is dead; even the loftiest ideals remain lifeless without action. Action matters because it is where faith and willpower meet reality. As the old saying goes, "You cannot steer a parked car." Once you move, even clumsily, God can steer you, open new doors, and connect you with resources you never anticipated.

From Intention to Impact: Bridging the Gap

Intention without impact leaves us feeling incomplete. We yearn not just for inspiring visions, but for real fruit tangible change in our lives, families, ministries, and businesses. Moving from intention to impact requires a willingness to risk, fail, and try again. Many biblical heroes realized that the cost of inaction was far greater than the risk of stepping out.

Take Nehemiah, who, despite fear of the king's wrath, voiced his concern about Jerusalem's walls (Nehemiah 2). His bold question, "Why shouldn't I be sad?" led to safe passage, resources, and the rebuilding of Jerusalem.

Had Nehemiah merely intended to help, the city might have remained in ruins. Similarly, Esther contemplated the danger of breaking palace protocol, knowing it could mean death. Yet silence would have meant annihilation for her people. She chose to act, and her courage had an impact that still echoes through history.

These timeless examples remind us: when urgency meets conviction, action unlocks deliverance and progress.

The Cost of Inaction

Before diving into strategies for decisive action, we must confront what's at stake when we fail to move. Missed opportunities loom large; doors open for a season, and like the Israelites on the edge of the Promised Land, prolonged hesitation can mean forfeiting a window of favor. Confidence also erodes with every challenge we shrink from; each missed moment chips away at our belief in ourselves and in God's guidance.

Beyond that, inaction stunts potential. God desires to use us to bless others and failing to act impacts not only personal growth, but the lives connected to our purpose.

King Saul is a sobering example chosen and anointed yet crippled by indecision and fear of public opinion. His procrastination and partial obedience led to a tragic downfall, proving that when leaders fail to act courageously, entire communities suffer. The same principle applies in our families, workplaces, and ministries today.

Overcoming Barriers to Bold Action

Even when we recognize the cost of inaction, mental and emotional barriers can still paralyze us. Among the most common obstacles is the fear of failure the worry that you'll be humiliated, lose resources, or let others down.

Yet failure is rarely final. David, tending sheep and facing lions and bears, risked much in obscurity before standing boldly before Goliath. Missteps are inevitable but are better seen as learning experiences rather than verdicts on your worth.

Another obstacle is perfectionism: the belief that everything must be perfectly in place before starting. But 2 Corinthians 12:9 reminds us that God's strength is made perfect in our weakness.

Imperfect beginnings often lead to refined outcomes over time. Likewise, limited vision can hinder action when we underestimate what God can do through us. Ephesians 3:20 assures us that He can do "immeasurably more than all we ask or imagine" a reminder to think beyond our immediate circumstances.

Finally, the comfort trap often keeps us stuck, as we prefer familiar discomfort to unknown possibilities. Yet growth rarely happens in the safety of the nest. Rehearse a vision of what could be and remember the biblical figures who soared by leaving comfort behind.

A practical step: identify the barrier that resonates most with you. Write it down, pair it with a Scripture or promise that counters it, and bring it to prayer, asking God to rewire your responses.

Examples from the Modern World

In today's world, examples abound of those who chose bold action over fearful hesitation. Truett Cathy, founder of Chick-fil-A, took a remarkable stand in closing his restaurants on Sundays, an unusual decision in the fast-food industry. Critics called it foolish, but Cathy's faith-driven commitment to rest and worship fostered a strong corporate culture, leading Chick-fil-A to top sales-per-restaurant rankings.

Similarly, David Green of Hobby Lobby faced intense cultural and legal backlash for faith-based decisions, yet he remained unwavering. His bold stance protected his conscience and demonstrated how conviction-driven action can influence corporate policy and inspire others.

Closer to home, consider our Nigerian friend who, facing educational and financial struggles, boldly launched a poultry business to fund his schooling. He risked failure on multiple fronts, but by stepping into action, he discovered new income streams, resilience, and entrepreneurial wisdom that shaped his future.

In each case, the individuals faced real risks, yet by "taking the bull by the horn," they turned potential setbacks into stepping stones powerful reminders that faith-centered boldness often yields remarkable results.

Steps to Take the Bull by the Horn

Taking bold action begins by clarifying your "why." Knowing your motivation whether rooted in God's calling, a passion to solve a social issue, or a desire to break generational cycles provides the anchor you'll need when challenges arise.

Next, set SMART goals: Specific, Measurable, Achievable, Relevant, and Time-bound objectives. Replace vague aspirations like "start a business" with clear plans such as "register my business by month's end" or "secure a part-time job by a set date to finance my startup."

Embracing imperfect starts is vital. No one begins fully equipped. David's first public challenge was Goliath, but his private victories over lions and bears prepared him. Start small if needed pilot your idea, volunteer in a related field, or host a single event before launching a full conference. Momentum builds through action.

Alignment with accountability also strengthens boldness. Surround yourself with mentors and peers who understand your vision. As Solomon wisely noted in Ecclesiastes 4:9–10, "Two are better than one... if either of them falls, one can help the other up." Regular check-ins help you stay on course.

Finally, adapt and persevere. Even the best-laid plans meet obstacles. Like Daniel who pivoted under various kings, or Paul who adjusted his missionary routes, those who succeed learn to modify methods without abandoning their mission. Taking the bull by the horn demands not just courage to start but resilience to continue.

Balancing Boldness and Wisdom

Stepping out boldly doesn't mean acting rashly. The Book of Proverbs consistently lauds wisdom, urging believers to seek understanding, plan diligently, and heed wise counsel. Boldness and wisdom are meant to work together: wisdom discerns the right bull to grab, while boldness actually grabs it. Some tension will always remain overthinking can paralyze you, while impulsiveness can lead to unnecessary harm. The sweet spot is an informed, prayerful courage.

Biblical checkpoints help anchor this balance. Daniel, for instance, prayed thrice daily even under normal circumstances, and likely even more when facing crises or major decisions. Proverbs 15:22 reminds us that "plans fail for lack of counsel, but with many advisers, they succeed." And sometimes, God provides confirmation through Scripture, prophetic words, or a deep, unshakable peace as described in Philippians 4:When boldness and wisdom unite, you move forward with a confidence that is neither naïve nor passive.

The Spiritual Fuel for Bold Action

The ultimate fuel behind decisive action is a deep spiritual conviction a sense that your steps align with God's purpose. Romans 8:31 powerfully asks, "If God is for us, who can be against us?" When you are convinced of divine backing, external obstacles lose much of their intimidating power.

David exemplified this mindset when he declared to Goliath, "You come against me with sword and spear...but I come against you in the name of the Lord Almighty."

His courage came from faith, not physical might. Daniel refused to let decrees, or the threat of the lion's den deter him from praying and remaining true to his convictions. Esther, facing tremendous personal risk, voiced her resolve with, "If I perish, I perish."

Modern parallels abound. Tim Tebow kneeling in prayer during NFL games or Bethany Hamilton returning to surfing after a shark attack weren't acts of brash defiance, they were expressions of deep, faith-rooted conviction. Similarly, your spiritual "why" might center around launching a ministry, building a business anchored in kingdom values, or simply living with integrity in a corrupt environment. Rooted in God's character, bold action transcends ambition and becomes partnership with divine purpose.

Dealing with Critics and Adversity

Bold decisions almost inevitably attract critics. You may face accusations of arrogance, recklessness, or disloyalty to traditional norms. It's important to remember that even Jesus, who embodied perfect love, encountered intense hostility from religious leaders. If He faced resistance, we shouldn't be surprised when our bold steps stir opposition.

However, distinguishing constructive feedback from cynicism is crucial. Wise mentors may offer critiques that sharpen and refine your approach, while others will project their fears onto you, aiming to keep you "safe." Stay teachable, but resilient.

Nehemiah's story is a perfect example. He faced ridicule from Sanballat and Tobiah but refused to be derailed. Instead, he prayed, pressed on, and completed the rebuilding of Jerusalem's wall. Critics can only define you if you let them. When you focus on your higher calling, adversity clarifies rather than confuses, sharpening your sense of mission and deepening your resolve.

Celebrating Incremental Victories

Bold action doesn't always produce immediate, sweeping changes. Often, progress is incremental the wall is rebuilt one stone at a time, and the orchard grows one seedling at a time. Celebrating these small wins reinforces the habit of moving forward.

In 1 Samuel 7:12, Samuel raised a stone named "Ebenezer," saying, "Thus far the Lord has helped us." Marking micro-milestones fosters gratitude and reminds you of God's faithfulness, creating momentum for future progress.

Sharing testimonies, whether it's landing your first client, overcoming a technical challenge, or conquering a personal fear, not only reinspires you but also encourages others. The spirit of testimony builds a communal environment of "Yes, we can!"

At home, you could keep a simple journal or chart to track small weekly achievements. If you finish a chapter of a book project, overcome a personal hurdle, or secure an important meeting, pause to celebrate. Acknowledging these steps cements the action habit into your lifestyle and keeps your spirit fueled for the larger battles ahead.

A Word on Endurance

Taking the bull by the horn is not a single act. Often, it's repeated daily in small ways: stepping up to lead a meeting, confronting a toxic behavior in yourself or others, or introducing your faith in a setting where it's met with skepticism. Over time, these daily acts accumulate.

But endurance is key. Galatians 6:9 warns, "Let us not become weary in doing good, for at the proper time we will reap a harvest if we do not give up." The final harvest belongs to those who keep taking action even when results stall.

Endurance Tools

- ☐ Regular Self-Review: Evaluate what's working, what isn't, and where adjustments are needed.
- ☐ Community Support: As always, accountability partners, mentors, or small groups can pray you through seasons of discouragement.
- ☐ Rhythms of Rest: Even the boldest efforts need Sabbath intervals to recharge physically, mentally, and spiritually.

Endurance is the spine that holds your bold actions upright when the storms intensify.

Conclusion: Act Now, Rise Higher

We are all at risk of drifting back into inertia resting on knowledge instead of deploying it. But this book's rallying cry, "Don't Chicken Out, Eagle In," demands not just understanding but execution.

From David to Esther, from corporate leaders to our Nigerian friend, the pattern is clear: those who act in faith, with humility and courage, see transformation that surpasses their expectations. God's power often meets us *in motion*, not before we move.

Practical Reflection

Identify One Area where you've hesitated be it launching a project, confronting a challenge, or sharing your faith.

Write a Specific Action you can take this week. Include a date, a time, and the resources you need.

Pray Boldly: Ask God for courage, wisdom, and clarity. Stand on promises like Philippians 4:13 ("I can do all this through Him who gives me strength").

Execute without waiting for perfect conditions. Start small if you must but start.

Review and Celebrate: At week's end, note what went right, what can improve, and how God showed up.

Remember, taking the bull by the horn is not about recklessness. It's about recognizing that fear and complacency rob you and those you could bless of the breakthroughs God intends.

Imagine if the biblical heroes had remained in the realm of good intentions! David would never have slain Goliath, Daniel's integrity might have stayed hidden in private devotions, and Esther's people might have perished. But each time they took bold steps, divine favor and human bravery intertwined.

DON'T CHICKEN OUT, EAGLE IN

So, let the next step be your defining moment. The bull stands before you, formidable but not invincible. Armed with faith, guided by wise counsel, and resolved that inaction is no longer an option, you can engage the challenge head-on. Whether it's in ministry, business, family, or personal development, let boldness mark your path. You're not alone your story, like those of scriptural and contemporary heroes, is part of a tapestry God is weaving for His glory and your good.

The storm winds might blow, but as an eagle leverages those gusts to soar higher, so can you harness the energy of action to rise above any obstacle. The time to plan is not over, but it's time to move from planning to performance.

As you do, watch how God multiplies your efforts and surprises you with favor. After all, you were never meant to stay on the sidelines. Embrace the swirl of possibility, fling yourself into the fray, and proclaim: I will take the bull by the horn and by God's grace, I will prevail.

CHAPTER 11

FAITH IN THE STORM:

EMBRACING GOD'S STRENGTH

If there is one certainty in life, it's that storms will come. They crash against our carefully laid plans, threaten our sense of security, and test the depth of our convictions. From financial collapses to health crises, relationship upheavals to global pandemics, these tempests remind us how little control we truly have.

Yet in the biblical narrative and in countless testimonies today we see that storms can become the very crucible where faith is forged. Chapter 11 brings us face-to-face with the question: When the winds howl and the waves tower, will we yield to fear, or will we discover a deeper reliance on God's strength?

DON'T CHICKEN OUT, EAGLE IN

In earlier chapters, we examined how biblical figures overcame monumental challenges, how transitions can become catalysts for transformation, and how decisive action propels us forward. Now we focus on the inner posture that sustains us during life's fiercest battles: faith in the storm.

This chapter explores why adversity often accelerates spiritual growth, how trust in God can be both our anchor and our wings, and how to stand firm when there seems to be no visible end to the chaos. From David's psalms of lament to the steadfast testimonies of modern believers, we'll see that faith doesn't just help us survive storms it can lift us into a realm of peace and purpose we never imagined.

Storms as a Testing Ground for Faith

Throughout Scripture, storms and turbulent waters serve both symbolically and literally to illustrate divine power and human frailty. Think of the disciples on the Sea of Galilee, panicking while Jesus slept in the boat (Mark 4:35–41). Their fear exposed the limits of their faith.

Yet, once Jesus calmed the winds and waves, they marveled, "Who is this, that even the wind and the sea obey Him?"

Storms force us to confront uncomfortable truths. We are reminded of our limitations—realizing that we cannot master or predict every outcome, no matter how hard we try. Simultaneously, we are drawn to recognize God's sovereignty, seeing that the storms that overwhelm us pose no threat to Him. At the heart of every storm lies a choice: will we fight in our own strength, or will we trust in a power beyond ourselves?

Like the disciples, we may discover that when earthly anchors fail, it is God's presence that becomes our deepest and most unshakable security.

Biblical Threads: Trusting God Amid the Tempest

Two powerful biblical stories reinforce how storms refine and reveal faith.

In Matthew 14:22–33, the Apostle Peter steps out of a boat into a raging sea. For a few miraculous moments, he walks on water. His courage to step out demonstrates that real faith is not forged in comfort zones.

Peter dared to do what others would not. Yet, when he shifted his focus from Jesus to the surrounding storm, he began to sink teaching us that focus determines outcome. Even then, Peter found rescue in Jesus' outstretched arm, reminding us that failure isn't final when we allow God to catch us and lift us again.

Similarly, Jonah's story paints a vivid picture of trust, rebellion, and redemption. Jonah fled from God's command, boarding a ship heading the opposite direction from his calling. A violent storm erupted, threatening everyone on board. It became clear that Jonah's disobedience was the root cause. Cast overboard, he found unexpected mercy in the belly of a great fish (Jonah 1–2).

Jonah's experience shows that storms can serve as wake-up calls, revealing areas of rebellion or avoidance that we must confront. His prayer from the depths is a plea of surrender, teaching that even in dire circumstances, hope remains when we turn back to God. Most importantly, Jonah's journey affirms that God can redeem even self-inflicted storms, offering second chances to fulfill our purpose.

In both accounts, storms become a stage for profound encounters with the Divine. Whether the chaos stems from external circumstances or our own missteps, storms direct our eyes upward toward the One who reigns above every gale.

Modern Examples: Faith Under Fire

Today's world offers powerful testimonies of faith refined through storms.

Bethany Hamilton's life changed forever at age thirteen, when a shark attack claimed her arm. What could have been a career-ending tragedy instead became a launchpad for deeper trust in God. Refusing to let fear or discouragement define her, Bethany returned to professional surfing, inspiring millions. Her storm of physical disability led to a greater platform of hope, showing how faith can transform tragedy into triumph.

Tim Tebow faced relentless media scrutiny and professional uncertainty, where his outspoken Christianity often overshadowed his athletic achievements. Critics claimed his style didn't fit the NFL and that his faith was too controversial. Yet Tebow met criticism not with bitterness but with prayer, charitable work, and an unwavering positivity that showed storms of public judgment can refine, not destroy, a person's mission.

Similarly, our Nigerian friend's journey from financial struggles to entrepreneurship reflects faith under fire. Losing his mother, facing academic challenges, and launching businesses abroad brought wave after wave of uncertainty. Yet every storm opened unexpected paths through last-minute opportunities, divine provision, and hard-won perseverance. Each trial deepened his conviction that God's strength is most visible when human strength runs dry.

In all three stories, the storms did not vanish overnight. Instead, each individual chose to root themselves more deeply in God's promises. Their perseverance was not the absence of hardship, but the refusal to let hardship define them.

Why Storms Often Deepen Faith

Storms are often the soil where true faith grows. They strip away illusions of control. In everyday life, we often live as though we can predict or manage every outcome.

Yet a financial crisis, health scare, or unexpected betrayal quickly shatters that illusion, forcing us to choose between despair and deeper trust in God's sovereignty.

Storms also reveal authentic dependence. Times of peace can subtly foster self-reliance, but real adversity exposes whether our trust in God is genuine or merely lip service. Desperate prayers and raw seeking tend to emerge only when human solutions fail.

Furthermore, storms grow endurance. James 1:2-4 exhorts believers to consider it pure joy when facing trials because testing produces perseverance and maturity. Trials aren't about punishment—they are about preparation, strengthening spiritual muscles for future assignments.

Finally, storms build empathy and future ministry. Those who endure adversity often become the very ones who can comfort others. As 2 Corinthians 1:3-5 says, those comforted by God during hardship are equipped to comfort others. Our own pain, when redeemed by God, can become the lifeline someone else desperately needs.

Choosing Faith Over Fear

Identifying Fear's Voice

Fear has a vocabulary: *"What if you fail?" "You can't handle this." "God won't come through."* Recognizing these whispers helps us counter them with truth.

Psalm 56:3 says, "When I am afraid, I put my trust in you." The psalmist doesn't deny fear but redirects it.

Declaring God's Promises

Faith gains traction when it is anchored in concrete promises. Scripture reminds us that God's provision is certain: "And my God will meet all your needs"

(Philippians 4:19). His presence is unwavering: "I will never leave you nor forsake you" (Hebrews 13:5). His peace is accessible: "Do not be anxious about anything... present your requests to God. And the peace of God... will guard your hearts" (Philippians 4:6–7).

By declaring these truths aloud, we shift our internal narrative from panic to trust, reorienting our spiritual posture toward God's unchanging character rather than the immediate force of the storm.

Action Rooted in Faith

Faith demands more than mental agreement it calls for decisive action. Noah built an ark without seeing rain; David ran toward Goliath rather than shrinking back; believers today are called to launch ventures or ministries despite daunting odds.

Fear shrinks from risk, but faith moves forward, saying, "I'll obey anyway," trusting that God's power will manifest in the process.

Practical Ways to Stand Firm in the Storm

Standing firm requires intentional spiritual habits. Daily prayer and worship are essential, as storms easily drain emotional reserves. Choosing to praise God even when emotions rebel shifts focus from the magnitude of the problem to the greatness of the Lord.

Resilience also thrives in community. Sharing burdens, requesting prayer, and allowing others to speak life into your situation provides crucial support. Recording testimonies and journaling answered prayers build a reservoir of faith, reminding you of God's faithfulness when new storms arise.

Oddly enough, serving others during personal crises can lighten your own burden. Giving your time, encouragement, or resources realigns priorities and broadens perspective, fulfilling the principle Jesus taught: "Give, and it will be given to you" (Luke 6:38).

Some battles require deeper spiritual discipline. Fasting or focused retreats can bring breakthrough, much like Jesus' wilderness fast prepared Him for temptation and ministry (Matthew 4). When everything external feels unstable, these practices ground us, reinforcing the eternal truth that storms are temporary, but God's promises endure.

Storms and God's Redemptive Power

One of the marvels of biblical faith is that God doesn't merely shield us from storms; He redeems them for His purposes. Joseph's brothers intended harm when they sold him into slavery, yet Joseph later proclaimed, "God intended it for good" (Genesis 50:20). Even the crucifixion the darkest storm in human history became the doorway to redemption for all mankind.

In our lives, storms can open unexpected doors. A job loss might birth an entrepreneurial calling or ignite a deeper passion for ministry. Hardship refines character, cultivating patience, humility, empathy, and endurance in ways comfort never could. And those who endure storms often emerge with heightened spiritual authority like David, who fought lions and bears before facing Goliath, developing faith that inspired a nation.

Acknowledging God's redemptive power doesn't trivialize suffering; it infuses hardship with hope. No storm is wasted in God's economy. If we yield to His shaping, every gust of adversity can propel us toward our divine destiny. Avoiding the Trap of Cynicism

When storms persist, the temptation to fall into cynicism grows. Some conclude that God doesn't care or that faith is futile. Job's wife, overwhelmed by her husband's suffering, urged him, "Curse God and die!" (Job 2:9). But Job chose a different path, maintaining his integrity and refusing to abandon trust.

Honest lament is valid, and the Psalms show that raw sorrow can coexist with unwavering hope. Faith isn't denial; it's the courageous choice to grieve and yet still declare God's goodness. Remembering others' journeys whether biblical or contemporary also fosters perspective. Testimonies of deliverance remind us that storms do end and that perseverance has a reward.

Most importantly, clinging to God's character steadies the soul. When circumstances defy explanation, we return to what we know: God is love, He is justice, He is mercy, and He is faithful. Holding fast to these truths keeps the roots of our faith anchored even when the surface is battered by relentless storms.

Cynicism grows from prolonged disillusionment, but it can be countered by consistent reminders of who God is and how He has acted throughout salvation history.

Navigating Long Storms: Patience and Perspective

Some storms pass quickly, but others linger, testing endurance over months or even years chronic illness, financial struggles, or enduring family conflicts. In these prolonged trials, patience and perspective become vital allies.

DON'T CHICKEN OUT, EAGLE IN

Rather than obsessing over an unseen finish line, it's important to embrace a day-by-day approach. Jesus taught, "Do not worry about tomorrow" (Matthew 6:34). Long storms require a manna-like dependence, trusting God to meet today's needs without borrowing tomorrow's troubles.

Specialized support can also be essential. Chronic challenges often require professional counseling, financial planning, or medical treatment. God frequently works through human experts as well as divine intervention.

Celebrating incremental progress becomes another life-giving practice. Noticing small improvements or moments of relief keeps hope alive. A heavenly perspective also proves critical.

Paul, despite lengthy imprisonments and afflictions, described them as "light and momentary troubles" compared to the "eternal glory" ahead (2 Corinthians 4:17). Shifting focus to eternity reframes earthly storms, reminding us that temporary suffering cannot eclipse everlasting promises.

Trusting God in prolonged adversity is more like running a marathon than a sprint. Like seasoned runners who "hit the wall" but press through to find second winds, believers can experience fresh surges of faith when endurance feels depleted.

The Role of Prayer and Spiritual Warfare

Storms often coincide with spiritual battles. As Ephesians 6:12 reminds us, our struggle isn't merely against flesh and blood. The enemy may exploit crises to sow doubt, division, or despair. Thus, deliberate prayer and sometimes spiritual warfare is essential.

Speaking Scripture aloud becomes a powerful weapon, following Jesus' example when He countered Satan's temptations with "It is written…" (Matthew 4:1–11). Wearing the full armor of God the belt of truth, breastplate of righteousness, shield of faith, and more (Ephesians 6:13–18) equips believers to stand firm when external chaos strikes. Spiritual discernment is also crucial; some storms have supernatural dimensions that require strategic, Spirit-led intervention.

Prayer isn't merely a coping mechanism; it's active engagement with divine power, a partnership with God that shapes outcomes and strengthens our hearts in battle.

DON'T CHICKEN OUT, EAGLE IN

Reflection: Our Nigerian Friend's Take on Faith in the Storm

Amid multiple challenges family responsibilities, academic hurdles, cross-cultural adjustments our Nigerian friend repeatedly leaned on prayer, community, and the Word. Whenever finances ran thin or ventures teetered, he fought off despair by returning to biblical promises.

He recounts how seemingly impossible bills were paid and how unexpected mentors offered timely advice. His life exemplifies a vital truth: God's strength often appears in the darkest moments of the storm, not before. Refusing to give in to cynicism, he sowed seeds of faith diligently studying hard, pivoting business strategies, serving faithfully in church fellowships.

Adversity became the stage for God's faithfulness, forging spiritual muscles that remain even now in calmer seasons. He testifies that without those storms, his foundation of trust would not have been as deep or resilient.

Conclusion: Soaring Above, Not Escaping

Faith in the storm doesn't guarantee instant deliverance; sometimes the storm must simply run its course. But what faith does promise is an inner calm the world cannot replicate, and an assurance that God is at work even when the winds howl fiercest.

As we conclude, consider the eagle. Eagles don't flee storms they harness turbulent winds to soar higher. In the same way, our storms can become the very forces that elevate us if we choose faith over fear and trust God's strength to sustain us.

Practical Takeaways

Rather than denying the existence of the storm, acknowledge it. Denial prolongs fear. Identify the nature of your storm whether financial, relational, or emotional and bring it honestly before God in prayer. Cultivate faith disciplines such as daily devotion, worship, fellowship, and meditation on Scripture. Whether the skies are clear or cloudy, deep roots are necessary.

Refuse isolation. Invite trusted friends or mentors to walk with you through the storm; collective prayer and counsel can be the difference between sinking and standing firm. Stay alert for divine surprises unexpected resources, encouragements, or new opportunities that often arise amidst turmoil.

Anchor yourself firmly in God's nature. When everything else is shifting, hold fast to who God is: a

DON'T CHICKEN OUT, EAGLE IN

loving Father, a just King, a faithful Provider. Storms challenge our theology, but letting Scripture reaffirm God's attributes brings a confidence no trial can shake.

Remain teachable. Ask God what lessons He wants you to learn: refinement of character, better stewardship, or deeper compassion for others. Storms are classrooms disguised as chaos.

Moving Forward

In the next and final chapter, we'll pull everything together courage, resilience, decisive action, and enduring faith into a blueprint for bold living. Remember: storms aren't meant to drown you; they can elevate you, shaping you into someone who stands firm and points others to the God who calms seas.

As you face your own storms, take heart. The same God who sustained David, Daniel, Esther, and countless modern heroes stands beside you today, arms outstretched, ready to sustain and guide you to new heights.

Storms may rage, but they do not have the final word. Faith does. Trusting God in the tumult is not denial of reality; it's the courageous recognition that an unseen reality the faithfulness of our Creator is greater than any wave.

In that recognition, you will find the strength to persevere, the peace that surpasses understanding, and the vantage point of an eagle rising above the clouds. Let the world see you anchored in God's might, unswayed by fear, a living testimony that no storm can drown a soul rooted in divine strength.

DON'T CHICKEN OUT, EAGLE IN

CHAPTER 12

SOARING FORWARD:

A BLUEPRINT FOR BOLD LIVING

Every chapter in this book has been about rising above, refusing to bow to fear, and discovering the courage that's formed through faith, community, and decisive action. We've drawn lessons from David slaying Goliath, Daniel standing firm in Babylon, and Esther risking her life for her people.

We've watched eagles ascend using storm winds, harnessing the very force that would ground lesser birds. And we've seen modern reflections from Tim Tebow to Bethany Hamilton people who converted trials into testimonies. In each story, there's a common thread: a willingness to trust God, step into the unknown, and see adversity as an invitation to soar.

Now, at the culmination of these lessons, Chapter 12 focuses on synthesizing these principles into a blueprint for bold living. How do we walk out of these pages ready to take that next leap, face the next giant, or confront the next storm? This is your invitation to a new normal a life that defies timidity and rises with an eagle's perspective, confident in the God who called you to boldness.

A Recap of the Journey

Before we map out practical steps, let's briefly trace the ground we've covered and why it matters. We began by confronting the insidious whisper of fear, which often masquerades as caution or realism.

Throughout the book, we made it clear that acknowledging fear is not weakness; allowing it to dictate your decisions is. Biblical heroes felt fear but acted in faith a defining trait that set them apart.

Then we learned that standing firm and soaring higher is about resilience shaped by faith and discipline, not mere bravado. The eagle taught us that storms are not to be feared but harnessed, providing the updraft to new altitudes.

DON'T CHICKEN OUT, EAGLE IN

Purpose and perseverance emerged as themes that sustain us when progress is slow or the road is lonely. Our Nigerian friend modeled this truth in real life, showing how a deep sense of calling can fuel endurance through hardship.

We emphasized the importance of decisive action and faith in the storm. Plans and prayers must lead to bold movement; otherwise, they remain theoretical. Storms, though inevitable, are divine opportunities to deepen trust and emerge stronger. These principles converge into a life that refuses to "chicken out," choosing instead to "eagle in."

Embracing the "Don't Chicken Out, Eagle In" Mindset

The phrase "Don't Chicken Out, Eagle In" represents more than catchy words. It is a mindset where fear is recognized but not allowed to lead. It doesn't advocate reckless confidence but rather a holy boldness that recognizes adversity as a stage for God's grace.

This mindset merges humility with confidence. We don't pretend to have all the answers or resources; we simply trust the One who does. True confidence stems not from our own abilities but from aligning with God's power and purpose. That kind of faith acts. It starts businesses, faces giants, and steps out onto stormy waters, believing that God will meet us there. Every step weakens fear's grip and strengthens a lifestyle of courage.

Living as an eagle is never self-centered. David's faith stirred a nation. Daniel's integrity impacted empires. Esther's courage saved a people. Your bold steps are not just about you they become sparks of inspiration that awaken courage in others.

From Knowledge to Practice: Making It Personal

Putting these lessons into action begins with self-assessment and prayer. Identify the giants in your life financial burdens, strained relationships, career uncertainties. Where have you been shrinking back in fear? What's at stake if you do nothing? Let the Holy Spirit reveal what may be hidden behind busyness or excuses.

Then, move to action. Set faith-driven goals that are both measurable and spiritually aligned. Break them into smaller, manageable tasks to build momentum. Find someone to hold you accountable, celebrate milestones, and keep your resolve strong. Every step is both a victory and a seed of greater faith.

DON'T CHICKEN OUT, EAGLE IN

To sustain bold living, nurture spiritual practices. Daily scripture realigns your heart with truth. Regular prayer keeps you in tune with divine guidance. Community offers encouragement, correction, and strength. Fasting or retreating in critical moments brings clarity and renewal. These habits build the strong wings needed for consistent flight.

Navigating Resistance and Adversity

Boldness will be tested. Critics will arise family members uncomfortable with your growth, colleagues questioning your values, and that persistent inner critic whispering doubt. Respond with obedience to God over approval from others. Root your identity in His love, not public validation. Even Jesus faced skepticism from His own hometown.

Expect spiritual resistance as well. Bold initiatives often stir spiritual warfare. Equip yourself with truth, faith, and prayer partners who will cover you as you advance. And remain adaptable. Sometimes a closed door is God's redirection, not rejection. Like Daniel or Paul, learn to pivot without losing purpose.

Strengthening Others as You Soar

Soaring eagles inspire others. Every biblical hero's victory echoed beyond their personal story. Likewise, your journey can encourage family, friends, or even strangers watching from afar. Your faithfulness in storms becomes a testimony of what's possible through God.

Take time to mentor others. Be honest about your journey not just the triumphs, but the trials and lessons. Pray with those walking similar paths. Share the books, tools, and communities that helped you grow. Multiply your impact by mobilizing others to address needs in your church or neighborhood. When people see boldness paired with compassion, they are drawn to the source behind your strength.

Evaluating and Continuing the Journey

A blueprint gives direction, not perfection. Periodically step back and assess your growth. Have you gained confidence? Taken difficult steps? Are there patterns holding you back? If so, adjust with grace. God is never short on mercy. What matters is your willingness to return and realign.

Prepare for new storms. Growth invites fresh challenges. Stay alert, not anxious. The same God who brought you this far will continue to lead. Watch for the signs, stay in tune with His voice, and let adversity become your next altitude.

DON'T CHICKEN OUT, EAGLE IN

Sustaining a Lifestyle of Bold Faith

This life of boldness is not about occasional acts of bravery; it's about faithful consistency. The grand gestures may be rare, but daily obedience praying for a colleague, standing for truth, extending forgiveness builds a legacy of courage. Stay teachable. Stay humble. Stay visionary. Let God renew your purpose and expand your reach, but never forget the Source.

Final Reflections on Our Nigerian Friend's Legacy

The story of our Nigerian friend is a powerful reminder that God uses ordinary lives in extraordinary ways. From family responsibility to academic hardship, from entrepreneurial risk to spiritual leadership, he kept stepping forward. He acted not when things were ideal but when faith said move. And in doing so, he inspired others to believe again.

His life is not perfect. He is still evolving. But that's the point. Bold living is a continual journey of growth and surrender. His story is not just his it is a mirror of what's possible when anyone chooses to live by faith.

A Commission to Rise

As we close this book, hear this not as a farewell but a sending. The same Spirit who strengthened biblical giants now lives in you. Will you rise to the call? Will you let faith define your steps? You have everything you need: the promises of Scripture, the guidance of the Holy Spirit, the support of community, and the covering of grace. Your time is now. Start with what you have. Start where you are. Every act of faith matters.

Your Roadmap: Putting It All Together

As a final synthesis: Confront fear. Face giants boldly. Rise above storms. Leverage community. Navigate transitions. Take decisive action. Trust God in the storm. And soar forward.

Let these become habits, not just highlights. Let your life reflect what you've learned. Let boldness become your rhythm.

The Continual Call to "Eagle In"

The journey doesn't end here. New winds will rise. Giants will reappear. But each time, you'll be more prepared. Like the eagle, you were built for sustained ascent, not short sprints. Embrace the winds. Adapt. Grow. Soar again.

DON'T CHICKEN OUT, EAGLE IN

Concluding Charge: Rise and Shine

This is your charge: Don't Chicken Out, Eagle In. Let these words define how you see challenges, how you take risks, how you pray, how you lead. You are created in God's image. You are redeemed by Christ. You are empowered by the Spirit. You have no reason to live small.

Trust the design God has given you. Trust the currents He sends. Let Scripture anchor you. Let faith lift you. Spread your wings. Move boldly. Inspire others. Let your life shine with such clarity that others can't help but look up and believe that they, too, can rise.

Final Benediction

May the God who parted seas for Moses, who gave victory to David, who rescued Daniel from lions, who empowered Esther to save her people, and who has worked miracles through everyday people in modern times, also empower you. May you remember that you are called to a life of unwavering faith, dynamic service, and unstoppable hope. And may each storm, rather than push you down, become the very wind that lifts you to new heights just as the eagle uses the tempest for altitude.

Thus ends this book, but the real journey begins now, in your next choice, your next risk, your next prayer. Pick up the lessons, cultivate the practices, and carry this rallying cry in your heart: Don't Chicken Out, Eagle In. The sky awaits. Let your wings spread, let your faith rise, and let the world see that no storm is greater than the God who calls you to soar.

AFTERWORD

If you're closing these pages feeling stirred, don't let the fire fade. Mark a date on your calendar to review your goals, pray about your "next giant," or share your new insights with a mentor or small group. Remember, growth is continuous. Each day offers fresh winds that can propel you further into a bold, God-honoring life. It's time to rise.

CONCLUSION

A life of boldness always begins in the heart. It starts with a stirring sense that we are called to more than routine mediocrity a conviction that fear and comfort should never dictate our destiny. Over the preceding chapters, we've examined how David faced Goliath, how Daniel thrived in a lion's den, and how Esther risked her life for the sake of her people. In every instance, their actions sprang not from extraordinary human capacity, but from faith in an extraordinary God.

This book's central image the eagle rising on storm winds reminds us that adversity need not be our undoing. Instead, it can become the very force that lifts us higher. Eagles don't shy away from turbulent skies; they catch the currents to gain altitude. Likewise, fear should not convince us to hide. Instead, we can see difficulties as invitations to discover untapped strengths.

DON'T CHICKEN OUT, EAGLE IN

By choosing the "Don't Chicken Out, Eagle In" mentality, we learn that real courage doesn't come from wishing for smooth waters; it comes from trusting the One who rules the wind and the waves.

Our journey began with an honest look at how fear whether it's dread, doubt, or insecurity can masquerade as wisdom or realism, keeping us perpetually grounded. The tipping point to progress is recognizing that fear doesn't vanish by itself. It's neutralized by action and faith.

When David ran toward Goliath, it wasn't bravado it was a conviction that God was bigger than any giant. That same principle applies in modern contexts, whether you're starting a new business, confronting a toxic situation, or rebuilding a life after loss. Fear fades when confronted by unwavering trust in God's sufficiency.

We explored Daniel's steadfastness in an empire that tested his integrity and Esther's heroic willingness to stand in the gap for an entire nation. These biblical heroes modeled how resolve and faith converge in crisis moments. They didn't wait for perfect conditions; they trusted in a perfect God who can deliver.

From each story, we drew parallels to contemporary examples like Bethany Hamilton, who surmounted life-altering challenges, or Tim Tebow, who remained fearless under unrelenting scrutiny. Their experiences highlight that no storm be it criticism, tragedy, or uncertainty has the final say unless we let it. Storms either cripple us or propel us to new heights, depending on where we place our faith.

A pivotal element in this bold living is discovering a why that's bigger than ourselves. Purpose-driven perseverance transforms trials into fuel for transformation. It's not the absence of hardship that builds resilience, but the presence of a higher calling that motivates us to keep going.

Our Nigerian friend's path illustrated how financial strains, academic obstacles, and family duties became stepping stones, precisely because he was propelled by a deep sense of responsibility, faith, and vision.

But resolve alone isn't enough. Without decisive action, even the most profound calling remains dormant. "Taking the bull by the horn" taught us that knowledge must translate into action stepping out of the boat like Peter, stepping onto the battlefield like David, or stepping forward for an oppressed people like Esther.

Good intentions and thorough plans might give us a framework, but it's when we actually move that we see

DON'T CHICKEN OUT, EAGLE IN

God's power unfold. Action is where faith becomes tangible, where ideas become impact.

And storms will come moments that challenge our deepest beliefs, threaten our security, and expose our frailties. Yet, as we learned, faith in the storm is not naive optimism; it's a solid anchor rooted in God's unchanging character.

Trusting God amid chaos transforms terror into a testimony. Whether it's a health crisis, job loss, or relational conflict, adversity compels us to choose: either fixate on the storm's fury or fix our eyes on the One who commands the wind and waves. Stories from biblical times to modern testimonies consistently show that adversity refines us, clarifies our priorities, and deepens our dependence on God.

Pulling all these threads together, we see a clear roadmap: Acknowledge fear honestly by naming what scares you and bringing it into the light of Scripture and prayer. Stand firm in your identity, recognizing that you are created by God and empowered by His Spirit. No threat can diminish that truth. Lean into your purpose. Clarify your life's "why" a divine calling, a passion to serve, or a family responsibility.

Purpose sustains perseverance when emotions waver. Take action. Move from intention to execution. Even small steps, done in faith, carry exponential impact. Surround yourself with a supportive community. Healthy fellowship provides prayer support, accountability, and synergy. We were never meant to tackle giants alone. And finally, trust God's strength in the storm. Embrace that storms can elevate you. Surrender to God's leading, and allow adversity to refine, not define, you.

These aren't isolated principles; they are threads of a single tapestry that spells out bold living in the face of fear. At every juncture, the overriding message is the same: Don't Chicken Out, Eagle In.

If you've walked through these chapters thinking, "I want this but don't know if I can sustain it," remember that David wasn't always a giant-slayer he started as an unknown shepherd.

Esther was an orphan before she became a queen. Daniel was a captive before he rose to influence. Their transformations weren't about self-made success but about responding to God's call, day by day, choice by choice.

DON'T CHICKEN OUT, EAGLE IN

Your next chapter might be stepping into an uncharted career path, repairing a broken relationship, or finally pursuing that God-birthed dream you've shelved for years. Whatever it is, your story matters. The storms you face, the giants you challenge, and the leaps of faith you take aren't in vain. They're part of a greater narrative in which God's strength is showcased through human weakness.

As you close this book, do so with a heart ready to open new doors. Practice the daily disciplines of prayer, Scripture, and fellowship. Challenge yourself to speak life and possibility where fear once dictated silence. Dare to dream bigger, attempt what seems impossible, and serve in ways that stretch your capacity.

No one is invincible but when aligned with God's purpose, ordinary individuals can become extraordinary witnesses of love, faith, and fortitude. Whether you find yourself on a literal battlefield, a corporate boardroom, a hospital bedside, or a quiet place of personal struggle, you're called to rise. You might have to face storms, but you can do so with wings outstretched, capturing the currents that elevate you beyond what you thought possible.

So, dare to believe. Dare to act. And dare to see what miracles unfold when you simply refuse to "chicken out," choosing instead to "eagle in." Your best chapters may lie just on the other side of that bold decision, that surrendered prayer, that unwavering stand. Let the world see you soar and let them witness the God who empowers such flight.

ABOUT THE AUTHOR

Pelumi Opeyemi Oyeboade is a Nigerian-born Bible teacher, speaker, and leadership coach whose life and work embody the very message of this book: courageous faith in the face of adversity. With a voice that resonates across pulpits, classrooms, boardrooms, and mentoring circles, Pelumi has spent more than a decade equipping believers to overcome fear, break limitations, and pursue God-given purpose with bold, unwavering conviction.

His story begins not in comfort or privilege, but in the resilient soil of personal struggle. Raised in a faith-filled home and later tested by the early loss of his parents, Pelumi experienced firsthand the storms that threaten to paralyze vision. Yet it was through those very trials—academic setbacks, financial strain, and personal loss—that his eagle mindset was born. Instead of succumbing to fear, he chose to harness adversity as a training ground for leadership, spiritual depth, and impact.

Over the years, Pelumi has emerged as a trusted mentor to emerging leaders, pastors, students, and entrepreneurs. His approach is grounded in Scripture but never abstract. Known for his vivid storytelling and real-life applications, he helps his audience translate biblical insight into courageous action. Whether he's teaching on how David faced Goliath, or helping a young professional navigate career transitions, Pelumi's message remains the same: don't settle for the ground when you were born to soar.

He is also deeply committed to the next generation. As a leadership coach, he trains others not just to succeed, but to do so with integrity, conviction, and spiritual clarity. He believes in multiplying leaders who

DON'T CHICKEN OUT, EAGLE IN

are equipped to serve their families, communities, churches, and nations with both passion and purpose. In many ways, this book is an extension of his coaching and discipleship work a field manual for living boldly in a fear-dominated world.

Don't Chicken Out, Eagle In is more than a title for Pelumi; it is a personal anthem forged in the crucible of hard choices and divine grace. The imagery of the eagle rising on storm winds is not just metaphorical—it captures his lived experience. From his early struggles with mathematics after the death of a parent, to the risks of launching entrepreneurial ventures while still in school, to the cross-cultural journey of building ministry and business abroad, Pelumi has consistently chosen faith over fear. His own story, woven subtly throughout the pages of this book, is proof that eagles are not born in the absence of storms, but in their midst.

A gifted communicator with an eye for transformation, Pelumi has spoken at conferences, churches, and mentorship forums across multiple continents. He is especially passionate about the global African diaspora, believing that our setbacks can become springboards, and that our faith can reshape not only our own destinies but also the futures of our communities. His work speaks deeply to those navigating change be it relocation, reinvention, or resurrection of buried dreams.

Behind the public platform lies a man of deep devotion and quiet discipline. Pelumi is a lifelong student of Scripture, a spiritual son to seasoned mentors, and a man whose personal prayer life anchors his public voice. His writing is as authentic as his preaching accessible yet profound, practical yet prophetic.

He is married to Abiodun Oyeboade, his partner in life and ministry, whose love and faith have strengthened his wings during seasons when fear tried to clip them. Together, they champion a message of hope, healing, and holy ambition for a generation longing to rise.

This is not just a book about overcoming fear. It's a lived testimony from someone who has refused to "chicken out" when everything around him said to quit. Through his words, coaching, and example, Pelumi calls you not to admire boldness from afar but to embrace it from within.

If you're looking for someone to stir your faith, sharpen your vision, and provoke you to act when the stakes are high, you've found that guide in Pelumi Opeyemi Oyeboade. And if you're ready to stop playing

DON'T CHICKEN OUT, EAGLE IN

small and start rising into your God-given identity, then you've picked up the right book.

Because with Pelumi leading the charge, one thing is certain: you will not leave this journey unchanged.

www.ingramcontent.com/pod-product-compliance
Lightning Source LLC
Chambersburg PA
CBHW032223080426
42735CB00008B/695